Effective Fundraising

2nd edition

Ben Wittenberg and Luke FitzHerbert

dsc
directory of social change

Published by the Directory of Social Change (Registered Charity no. 800517 in England and Wales)

Head office: Resource for London, 352 Holloway Rd, London, N7 6PA

Northern office: Suite 103, 1 Old Hall Street, Liverpool L3 9HG

Tel: 08450 77 77 07

Visit www.dsc.org.uk to find out more about our books, subscription funding websites and training events. You can also sign up for e-newsletters so that you're always the first to hear about what's new.

The publisher welcomes suggestions and comments that will help to inform and improve future versions of this and all of our titles. Please give us your feedback by emailing publications@dsc.org.uk.

It should be understood that this publication is intended for guidance only and is not a substitute for professional or legal advice. No responsibility for loss occasioned as a result of any person acting or refraining from acting can be accepted by the authors or publisher.

First published 2003
Reprinted 2006, 2011
Second edition 2015

ISBN 978 1 906294 61 8

British Library Cataloguing in Publication Data
A catalogue record for this book is available from the British Library

Cover and text design by Kate Bass
Typeset by Marlinzo Services, Frome
Printed and bound by Page Bros, Norwich

FSC
MIX
Paper from responsible sources
www.fsc.org   FSC® C023114

Luke FitzHerbert was one of DSC's
best loved and respected colleagues.
This book is dedicated to his memory.

About the series

This series of key guides is designed for people involved with not-for-profit organisations of any size, no matter how you define your organisation: voluntary, community, non-governmental or social enterprise. All the titles offer practical, comprehensive, yet accessible advice to enable readers to get the most out of their roles and responsibilities.

Also available in this series:

Charitable Incorporated Organisations, Gareth G. Morgan, 2013

Charitable Status, Julian Blake, 2008

The Charity Trustee's Handbook, Mike Eastwood, 2010

The Charity Treasurer's Handbook, Gareth G. Morgan, 2014

Minute Taking, Paul Ticher and Lee Comer, 2012

For further information, please contact the Directory of Social Change (see page viii for details).

Contents

About the authors

Luke FitzHerbert

Luke FitzHerbert was an extraordinary individual. He was best known for his work as the pioneer of guides to grant-making trusts, ground-breaking publications on the lottery and company giving, his regular contributions to the sector media and his tireless campaigning for greater transparency and probity in charitable activity. His publications have become required reading for all fundraisers and his fundraising training for thousands of organisations made him into a fundraising guru.

Luke's career path took many twists and turns before leading to his definitive role in the voluntary sector. Growing up in rural Ireland he went to Christchurch, Oxford to read history, via a spell in the Irish Guards. He worked variously in the print industry, as a volunteer skipper on a sailing training scheme and from 1975 to 1983 as a teacher in a west London comprehensive school. During these years he became the founder and chairman of the Brent River and Canal Society and it was that experience which embedded his passion for volunteering and the voluntary sector.

In 1983, Peter Jay, chairman of the National Council for Voluntary Organisations (NCVO), recruited Luke to help launch payroll giving in Britain. Shortly after in 1984, Luke approached Michael Norton, founder of DSC, and proposed the idea of compiling a directory of foundations which charities could use to help them to fundraise. As Deputy Director and later Co-Director of DSC, he went on to create and edit DSC's series of grants directories, and then do the same for directories on smaller and local trusts, and the *National Lottery Yearbooks*. These grants directories, invented by Luke, which include *The Guide to the Major Trusts* and *The Guide to UK Company Giving*, continue to be a mainstay of the on-going work of DSC.

Luke fearlessly said and wrote what he thought would be in the public interest, and he withstood pressure from the trusts to have their affairs remain closed from public scrutiny. By doing so, he singlehandedly modernised the practices of the philanthropic sector by encouraging more effective, efficient and accountable grant-making for social change and for the benefit of the poor. The sector is a better place for it.

Many people also knew Luke best as a trainer and benefitted from his direct and practical approach to raising money. His DSC fundraising courses, including Effective Fundraising and training on National Lottery outcome funding, were always in demand and his infectious energy, his passionate and principled iconoclasm and his love of the sector charmed everyone who met him.

Ben Wittenberg

Since joining DSC in 2003, Ben has had several roles, overseeing at various points, fundraising, website development, research, publishing, policy and campaigning. He has also been a regular columnist for *Charity Times*, writing on subjects ranging from the relationship between the government and the voluntary sector to good grant-making practices. He has raised more than £2 million in funding from a range of statutory, corporate, charitable and public sources. He has also run DSC training courses on fundraising from grant-making trusts, companies and government sources.

He led the development of DSC's funding websites (governmentfunding, trustfunding, companygiving and grantsforindividuals) which provide details of thousands of funders to voluntary sector organisations looking for funding to support their cause.

Prior to DSC, Ben was Project Coordinator for youth Charity Weston Spirit running projects for young disadvantaged people across the UK, including Reach for the Sky, a partnership with Sky Television. Before that he worked as a Project Leader for Royal and Sun Alliance.

He is an ILM Level 7 Executive Coach and has a BA (Hons) in European Studies and Politics, an MA in European Studies, and is a PGCE-qualified geography teacher.

In his spare time he sits on the committee of Southport and Waterloo Athletics Club, regularly running (and occasionally winning) marathons and ultramarathons all over the UK.

About the Directory of Social Change

The Directory of Social Change (DSC) has a vision of an independent voluntary sector at the heart of social change. The activities of independent charities, voluntary organisations and community groups are fundamental to achieve social change. We exist to help these organisations and the people who support them to achieve their goals.

We do this by:

- providing practical tools that organisations and activists need, including online and printed publications, training courses, and conferences on a huge range of topics;

- acting as a 'concerned citizen' in public policy debates, often on behalf of smaller charities, voluntary organisations and community groups;

- leading campaigns and stimulating debate on key policy issues that affect those groups;

- carrying out research and providing information to influence policymakers.

DSC is the leading provider of information and training for the voluntary sector and publishes an extensive range of guides and handbooks covering subjects such as fundraising, management, communication, finance and law. We have a range of subscription-based websites containing a wealth of information on funding from grant-making charities, companies and government sources. We run more than 300 training courses each year, including bespoke in-house training provided at the client's location. DSC conferences, many of which run on an annual basis, include the Charity Management Conference, the Charity Accountants' Conference and the Charity Law Conference. DSC's major annual event is Charityfair, which provides low-cost training on a wide variety of subjects.

For details of all our activities, and to order publications and book courses, go to www.dsc.org.uk, call 08450 777707 or email publications@dsc.org.uk.

Foreword

Effective Fundraising provides you with advice and information to help you raise money for your charity or project. Remember, though, that advice and information is not in itself enough. *You have to ask!* And you need to ask effectively. This means more than just filling in application forms or sending off proposals to trusts and foundations. It also means asking people to support you – people who can give you more than just money: they can give their time, their skills and expertise, and even reach out to their friends and their contacts, who might also like to help you.

Successful fundraising is all about being enthusiastic. Being enthusiastic about your project and what you want to achieve; being enthusiastic about asking, because you need to enthuse other people about what you want to do if you are to persuade them to support you.

Remember too that if you don't get the money you need, you can still do something. Have a Plan B, which is what you can do with less, as a first step; and have a Plan C, which is what you can do with no money at all. Getting going and doing something will show your determination and make fundraising in the future that much easier.

The book has been updated, now in its 2nd edition, to take account of legal, taxation and technology changes including new opportunities provided by social media and mobile technology and emerging methods of fundraising such as crowd funding and social lending. But the fundamentals of good fundraising don't change.

This book is imbued with the wise and practical advice of Luke FitzHerbert, a fundraising guru and mentor, and a cornerstone of the Directory of Social Change for many years. He inspired so many fundraisers to do more and do better and who fought for openness and transparency in the way that foundations and companies distributed their money. This book is dedicated to Luke's memory.

Michael Norton
May 2015

Acknowledgements

We are grateful to the following people and organisations for their kind permission to use case studies featuring their organisation and/or for reproducing their material(s).

David Kane at NCVO for his consent to reproduce the tables on pages 6 and 9, and figures 1.1 and 1.2 on pages 11–12.

The Research Team from Charities Aid Foundation for permission to reproduce the figures on pages 11–12.

The material on page 25 is adapted by the publisher from 'Education can lift whole communities out of poverty: Amna's story, 2015' with the permission of Oxfam GB, Oxfam House, John Smith Drive, Cowley, Oxford OX4 2JY UK www.oxfam.org.uk. Oxfam GB does not necessarily endorse any text or activities that accompany the materials, nor has it approved the content of the adapted text.

Robert Maltby, Communications and Marketing Manager at St Luke's Hospice Plymouth, for his help with and approval of the case study on page 36.

Ceri Edwards from the Institute of Fundraising for permission to reproduce guidance text on pages 15–16 and 40–41.

Manjuka and Steven Murdoch, Head of Fundraising, at the Karuna Trust for their permission to reproduce the case study text on page 51.

Clive Joyce, Editor of the *Hereford Times* for his approval to reproduce the newspaper article 'Charity helped by bingo nights', featured on page 58.

The MacRobert Trust for permission to reproduce the example guidelines on page 67.

Simon Pellew, Chief Executive at the Society of Analytical Psychology, for his permission to reproduce the case study text on page 79.

We are grateful to Pat Wallace, formerly of Winged Fellowship, for the case study on pages 18–19 and Mike Barford for the sales letter example on page 44, neither of whom we were able to locate but we believe would not have objected to the reproduction of these examples in this edition.

Further, we are grateful to the Robert Gavron Charitable Trust for its support for the writing of the first edition of this book and to Kay FitzHerbert for her help with the second edition.

1 The fundraising background

Fundraising and other forms of funding

There are lots of different ways for charities to raise the funds they need to serve their beneficiaries. Service delivery contracts, chargeable services to users, social investment, and the various activities that fall between them are all perfectly legitimate ways for charities to cover the costs of achieving their charitable aims.

They are not the focus of this book.

This book is about persuading people or institutions to give donations to your charity. A donation is a gift, usually made without the giver or donor expecting anything back in return, beyond the satisfaction of supporting what you do.

This book is also primarily about fundraising for charities (whether registered or not). It does not discuss raising money for the benefit of individuals, nor for private as opposed to public institutions such as, say, golf clubs or privately owned historic buildings. The box below explains what a charity is, and highlights the benefits of being registered as such.

Charitable status

If your organisation is not for profit and for the public benefit, it is likely to be a charity. If you have an income of £5,000 in a year or more, you should register with the Charity Commission if you are based in England or Wales, or the Office of the Scottish Charity Regulator (OSCR) in Scotland, or the Charity Commission for Northern Ireland (CCNI).

Each of the regulators has very simple and easy to follow advice on setting up and registering as a charity on their website, links to which are in the 'Useful organisations' section on page 99.

There is no law to prevent you from asking for money for a good cause – or indeed for any cause. You can get on with it without waiting for the formalities, though of course you must not say that your organisation is a registered charity if it is not. You will just need to convince those you ask that what you are doing deserves their support.

However, there are substantial advantages in formally registering as a charity.

1 It is seen as a seal of respectability

Some people and institutions, including many grant-making charities, either can or will give their money only to registered charities. If your group or organisation is too small to be registered, or have not yet got around to doing so, you will need to find a charity that is already registered to receive the donation or grant and then pass it on to you. This charity has to accept the responsibility for seeing that the money is indeed used for a genuinely charitable purpose. Various umbrella charities are used to performing this function. They include many national associations and also local councils of voluntary service (CVSs). For details of these, go to www.nacvs.org.uk.

For the benefits registration brings, supervision by the Charity Commission, OSCR and CCNI is quite light and, for charities with an income of under £10,000 a year (over half of all charities), it scarcely exists. If your charity's income exceeds £10,000 you will be required to submit an annual return form with basic information about your activities, and if your income exceeds £25,000 you will need to submit an annual report and independently audited or examined accounts.

Any investigations by any of the regulators are generally the result of an outside complaint.

2 You get council tax relief

Registered charities with their own premises can apply for an 80% reduction on this tax — a very important saving, which some local councils will top up to a 100% discount.

3 You become eligible for tax reliefs on donations

These are described later in this chapter (see page 13).

Should we fundraise for our charity?

Not necessarily. Donations or grants are just one way of funding what you do. Depending on what you are doing it may be more appropriate to charge for your work, like a charitable theatre company probably will. Maybe it makes more sense for your counselling service to be funded by a contract from your local authority, or even as a sub-contractor to another larger organisation. Perhaps your national association would be best funded by subscriptions from member organisations in return for the services you give them. Perhaps, like my own organisation, the Directory of Social Change (DSC), you are best suited to being a trading organisation – in our case, selling books like this to you! It is perfectly normal and proper for charities to be trading organisations though, of course, any profits must stay within the organisation.

But if you think that donations are an appropriate source for some or all of your funding, go for it. There is no shortage of money and there are people out there only too happy to support almost every cause if you can identify them, if you have a good case and if you ask them nicely.

However, if you, or a substantial proportion of your committee or trustees, have any doubts about it, perhaps you should not do it. If you would be embarrassed to be asked to support the cause yourself, then asking the public, let alone your family or friends, to pay for it will be uncomfortable and usually unsuccessful. No one should fundraise unless they are convinced that what they are doing is proper and appropriate.

Aren't there easier ways of getting money?

There may be. Before you decide on the best way to raise funds there are a lot of factors to consider. How much do you need to raise? Is it a one-off or ongoing need? What resources do you have at your disposal? If you are one person and need to raise £50,000, you may be more likely to succeed with an application to a grant-making charity than standing in the High Street shaking a collection tin.

If what you are trying to achieve fits closely with the current objectives of your local authority or a central government department, you may find a funding stream that is perfect for you, assuming you can navigate the application process and accept the associated terms and conditions.

But where there is no other funding available you will have to fundraise; and even when there may be a choice, having at least a substantial proportion of your own fundraised income may be hugely desirable.

> ### The Charity Commission register
>
> There are over 164,000 registered charities in England and Wales and perhaps as many again that are not registered. Usually charities do not register because they are too small but sometimes they are exempt from registration, like universities and churches. To get a feel for what is out there, you can browse the Charity Commission register on its excellent website at www.gov.uk/government/organisations/charity-commission. For a quick idea, you might go to 'Search the Register', choose 'Search by name' and 'Search by area', and enter the name of the place you live. You will probably be surprised by the number that show up. For example at the time of writing (April 2015) there are 34 charities that include the name of my home town of Formby and 866 based locally in Sefton.

What are the advantages of having fundraised income?

Having your own, unrestricted income is crucial to maintaining your freedom and independence. There are some strong arguments of principle around this, especially around how an over-reliance on grants or contracts where the priorities are set by an external body or organisation can lead to mission-drift. That is to say your organisation ends up doing what it can get funding for, rather than what it was set up for. However, from a practical perspective, the key thing you get from having your own funds is the independence to determine the best way to serve and support your beneficiaries.

Imagine a charity working with young people not in education, employment or training. They set up a project that gets the young people to work together to write, perform, record and edit ten-minute films about themselves and their hopes for the future. It's a great idea, and everyone's really excited about how it could engage the young people in thinking about their futures and build their confidence and self-esteem, while also giving them some technical skills. Except a few weeks in it's clear that it's not working. The young people are engaging with the planning, writing and performing, but not with the technical production. The youth team leaders are seeing big improvements in self-esteem and confidence right up to the point of performing their work, but it's disappearing for whatever reason during the production part of the project.

The young people and the youth team leaders want to ditch the film production element of the project, spend more time engaging with the issues they are discussing, and perform their work to an audience of their peers, friends and family instead.

If the costs of that work are being met with the charity's own money it is easy for them to adapt, to change what they are doing in the interests of the people they exist to support. In fact it would be irresponsible and doing a disservice to the young people not to do so. If, however, that work is being paid for under contract, with an agreement that the originally specified work will be carried out, it is much harder (if not impossible, depending on which body or organisation the contract is with) to respond mid-project in the interests of those young people.

Is getting grants 'fundraising'?

It depends, although the act of applying for grants is more often than not lumped into the wider category of fundraising. For me there is a distinction depending on the conditions that come with the grant. Core grants, grants that are given without conditions on how they can be spent (so long as they are spent in furthering the charity's aims) are becoming less and less common, especially from statutory sources. However, there are still around 700 grant-making charities listed on www.trustfunding.org.uk as giving core funding, with a combined grants total of over £450 million.

Generally, the more loosely a funder specifies what their grant can be spent on, the closer it is to a donation. The more specific they are, the closer it is to a payment for the delivery of services, which is something different. Most grants occupy the grey area in between.

The previous edition of this book urged caution with regard to grants, that they should be used for starting up new projects, but that it is better to develop more reliable income streams. I would echo that sentiment to a point, and I have certainly seen organisations that have been trapped in a cycle of repeatedly chasing short-term funding for what are inherently long-term needs. However, it is entirely possible to deliver real and lasting change with a mix of grant funding from different sources. A strong relationship with a good funder can be worth its weight in gold, especially in the early stages of an organisation or a project's development.

Fundraised money

Where does fundraised money come from?

The highest proportion comes from individuals. The table overleaf gives a breakdown of the main sources of income to charities in England and Wales. This is table is reproduced from *The UK Civil Society Almanac*, 2014 edition; the data is gathered from 2011/12.

	Voluntary	Earned		Total (1,000s)
	Donations and gifts	**Fundraising trading**	**Charitable trading**	
	Income freely given, usually as a grant, for which little or no benefit is received by the donor.	Selling goods and services specifically to raise funds for the charity	Selling charitable goods and services to individuals, government or others.	
Individuals	**£8,908.7**	**£3,490.4**	**£5,024.8**	**17,423.8**
The general public, excluding payments from charitable trusts set up by individuals	Individual donations (gross, including Gift Aid reclaimed); legacies; membership subscriptions without significant benefits.	Fundraising by charities where benefit is received in return, charity shop turnover, sales of merchandise, raffles and lotteries, fees for fundraising events.	Fees for services provided in pursuit of charitable objects; membership subscriptions with significant benefits; rent from property where providing accommodation is a charitable purpose.	
Statutory sources	**£2,560.3**	**£70.3**	**£11,026.1**	**£13,656.7**
Government and its agencies in the UK, the European Union and international governments	Funding grants; grants to charitable intermediaries.	Trading with public sector to raise funds.	Public sector fees; payments for contracted services.	
National Lottery distributors	**£492.0**			**£492.0**
	Grants from National Lottery distributors			
Voluntary sector	**£2,379.3**	**£81.7**	**£686.0**	**£3,147.0**
Charities such as grant-making trusts and foundations	Grants from charitable trusts and foundations; grants distributed by charitable intermediaries.	Trading with other charities to raise funds	Services provided under contract that are in line with the recipient charity's mission	
Private sector	**£933.0**	**£393.1**	**£496.3**	**£1,822.4**
Excluding payments from charitable foundations set up by businesses	Corporate donations and gifts in kind	Corporate sponsorship	Subcontracting, research, other services provided under contract	
SUB-TOTAL	**£15,273.2**	**£4,035.4**	**£17,233.2**	
Investment				**£2,707.3**
The proceeds generated from investments and cash balances				
TOTAL				**£39,249.1**

Kane et al. 2014, p. 37

How is the money given?

Most donations come from individual gifts, subscriptions or the sponsorship of fundraising events; as grants from trusts and foundations; or in grants or sponsorship from companies.

Individuals make donations while they are alive, as either single gifts or regular payments, in response to:

* personal or telephone request and discussion;
* letters (direct mail);
* advertising;
* word of mouth;
* taking part in your events.

Their money may come:

* as single payments, by cash, cheque, or online via your own website or an intermediary such as Just Giving;
* as membership subscriptions;
* as regular donations by direct debit or standing order;
* through buying tickets to events or for lotteries;
* from sponsoring your supporters' activities;
* as legacies, through people's wills when they die.

Grant-giving trusts and foundations, and some Lottery distributors, make grants to other charities, either from the income from their 'endowed' wealth or from money they have themselves raised from the public – BBC Children in Need and the like.

Community foundations

Community foundations are foundations that basically manage local pots of money on behalf of others. Rather than set up their own grant-making trust or foundation, individuals, families, businesses or other charities can give funds to their local community foundation, who will invest it along with other funds, and make grants with the proceeds in the same way as many other grant-makers. There are 48 community foundations in the UK, giving grants of around £65 million per year to a range of local causes (UK Community Foundations 2015).

Why is the total of grants from companies so small?

Many people are surprised to find how little of the total amount given to charities is donations from companies. The main reason for this public perception is our old friend, spin. So much active publicity is given to even modest corporate donations, that it has created a general but false public impression that companies are a major source of donations. They are not. However, because they are thought to be, many charities make quite unrealistic plans and offer equally unrealistic fundraising jobs in the area of corporate fundraising.

There is a view, held by DSC and others, that many companies simply do not give enough. That sentiment aside, when it comes to compiling meaningful data on how much companies actually do give, it is impossible to do so with any real certainty. The reporting by companies of their charitable donations varies wildly in its detail and accuracy. In the course of producing *The Guide to UK Company Giving*, DSC researchers regularly come across, what I'll generously refer to as, anomalies in reporting such as:

- counting donations from customers (i.e. at supermarket checkouts) as having been given by the company;
- stating the retail value of gifts in kind they have given, rather than the cost to them of giving them;
- valuing the salary, overhead and pension costs of staff that have been given time off to volunteer and adding that to the figure they report.

Further confusion comes from them reporting in completely different ways, using different methods to calculate their giving, and in some cases not recording it at all. Most of the figures on company giving also relate to big companies, giving big amounts of money to big (relatively speaking) charities. The countless small donations or gifts in kind from local businesses to the PTA for the raffle at the school summer fair, for example, aren't included anywhere because nobody is reporting them.

Putting aside the problems in company reporting of charitable giving, while the amount of donations given by companies is low, we should not forget or undervalue the support that companies can give charities in kind. Sometimes you just need to think a bit creatively about what they have that you need. (For more information on this, see Chapter 7 'Raising money from companies'.)

What causes do the public support?

There are two ways of looking at how much support the public gives to particular causes, the proportion of donors that give, and the proportion of the money given.

Cause	Proportion of donors giving	Proportion of total amount
Medical	33%	15%
Hospitals	30%	15%
Children	23%	11%
Animals	16%	5%
Overseas	14%	10%
Religious	14%	17%
Disabled	11%	4%
Health	8%	3%
Homeless	8%	2%
Schools	7%	4%
Elderly	6%	2%
Environment	5%	2%
Sports	3%	1%
Arts	1%	1%

Kane et al. 2014, p. 49

Medical research, hospitals and children consistently attract the highest number of donors, and along with religious causes attract nearly half of all the money donated by individuals. It is worth remembering, however, that although these figures provide some useful context, they are very broad categories, and even the lowest proportions of donations represent considerable sums of money. That only 2% of donated funds are for environmental causes could be seen as a challenge or a problem if that's the area you are fundraising in, until you realise that 2% actually represents over £300 million and you are only looking to raise £5,000 to conduct a wildlife population survey, for example.

It's also important not to see lists like this as being simply about public preferences. There are a range of factors that contribute to some causes being better supported by the public than others, not least the amount of money spent on fundraising campaigns by the largest charities in each area.

Britain's favourite big charities

Charity	Voluntary income	Legacy income	Total income
Cancer Research UK	372,705,312	142,456,707	536,557,309
The National Trust	66,836,000	44,688,000	435,916,000
OXFAM	129,700,000	15,000,000	385,500,000
The Save the Children Fund	103,704,000	13,088,000	283,748,000
British Heart Foundation	92,613,000	53,003	249,893,000
Barnardo's	43,385,000	15,015,000	245,182,000
The British Red Cross Society	109,600,000	20,300,000	200,100,000
Action for Children	20,189,000	5,060,000	197,962,000
Royal Mencap Society	12,969,000	6,200,000	196,584,000
The Royal National Lifeboat Institution	152,174,181	101,457,157	174,681,644
Age UK	50,051,000	23,463,000	167,655,000
The Salvation Army	101,765,000	41,697,000	162,208,000

CAF 2015

What methods of giving are used by donors?

The methods of people making donations have changed little since the previous edition of this book, which was published over ten years ago, although beneath the NCVO/CAF figures for cash giving in figure 1.1 are big increases in online giving. (Note that the percentages in figure 1.1 do not add up to 100% because donors give by more than one method. The data is from the 2012 edition; *UK Giving 2014*, published in 2015, does not include this information at the same level of detail.)

Figure 1.1 Methods of giving: proportion of donors and median amount, 2010/11

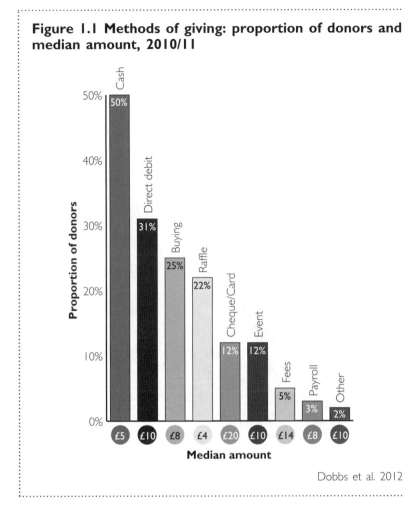

Dobbs et al. 2012

How much is the typical gift? Although there are very many small gifts, say of £5 or less, according to the NCVO/CAF figures shown in figure 1.2, they account for only a tiny amount of the total donated – around 6%. Over 40% of all the money donated is given in gifts of £100 or more. However, the median, or most common amount given in a month, is £10.

Figure 1.2 Share of total donations by size of donation, 2010/11

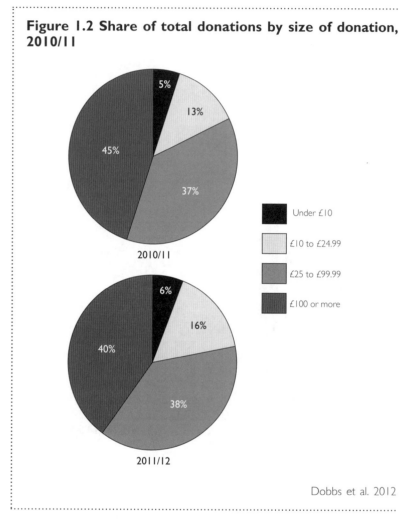

2010/11

2011/12

Under £10

£10 to £24.99

£25 to £99.99

£100 or more

Dobbs et al. 2012

Caution!

Generally speaking, it is very difficult to raise substantial money from small, single 'pocket money' donations. Most charities have to think of asking people for significant amounts, or small amounts regularly repeated, similar to what they have to pay for just about everything else of any significance.

However, the combination of social media and online giving can occasionally combine to give huge exposure to a cause, and subsequently generate significant amounts of income from very many small individual donations. During the summer of 2014 the Amyotrophic Lateral Sclerosis (ALS) Association launched their ice bucket challenge campaign to raise money and awareness for their cause. This basically involved people filming themselves pouring a bucket of ice over their head, posting it on social media, and nominating friends to do the same, and make a donation. Within a month ALS received $98.2 million, compared with the $2.7 million it had received in the same month the year before. Very quickly the Motor Neurone Disease Association (the British equivalent of ALS) started to benefit too, seeing its weekly donations figure jump from £200,000 to £2.7 million. Other charities including MacMillan Cancer Support and Water Aid quickly associated themselves with the craze, boosting their income to similar levels during the same period (Townsend 2014).

Tax reliefs

How can donations qualify for tax reliefs?

The principle of charitable tax relief is straightforward, even if the practice isn't. When a taxpayer (or tax-paying organisation such as most companies) gives money to a charity, the donor has already paid tax in order to have this amount available to give. This pre-paid tax can be reclaimed, giving the charity an extra 25p for every pound given. A donation of £100 therefore 'costs' the donor £100, but the charity receives £125.

If a donor pays a higher rate of tax, say 40%, they can also claim the difference between the higher and basic tax rate on their donation. Then a donation of £100 becomes a donation of £125 to the charity, which the donor can reclaim 20%, or £25 back themselves at a net cost to them of only £75.

You can register and set up to receive Gift Aid online at www.gov.uk-claim-gift-aid-online where there is more information about the specific requirements, but it is well worth registering if you are eligible.

Companies can get similar tax benefits, but grants from grant-making charities or from statutory organisations do not qualify as these are not taxpayers.

There are other tax concessions to do with payroll giving (see below) and with gifts of shares. For up-to-date information on the tax treatment of charities and charitable giving, refer to the HM Revenue & Customs website at www.gov.uk. You will find all sorts of useful advice here; in addition to a more detailed explanation of the Gift Aid scheme, there is more detailed information on how you can get VAT relief on particular charity purchases and on certain types of fundraising events. Legacies to registered charities are also free of inheritance tax.

How important are these benefits?

It's difficult to know how much influence they have on people's decisions to give money to charities. They may be more important in generating additional money from donations that would have been made anyway than they are in persuading people to give in the first place.

How difficult is it to organise the tax reclaims?

If you are claiming Gift Aid on a small number of donations it is quite simple once you have registered and downloaded the relevant templates. If you are receiving large numbers of individual donations it may be worth considering specific software which can make the claiming process easier, or even get one of the many agencies that specialise in Gift Aid to carry out that work for you. They will give you a quote and from then on, if you accept it, you just supply the information and the money will appear in your bank account. A full list of these is also available on the government website.

Should a small charity like ours get involved?

Yes, if you are going to get significant donations from taxpayers. But you can probably wait until you have the first of them in hand.

Payroll giving

Payroll giving is another tax-effective way of making donations. It is a system by which donors ask their employers for payments to the registered charity of their choice to be taken out of their pay each week or month.

How does it work?

To save each employer from having to make lots of small payments to different charities every week or month, employers simply send one payment for the total amount requested by all their employees to an intermediary or agent. They then reclaim the tax on all the money received each month and split up the total among all the different charities that have been nominated.

How much is given?

In 2013–14 1,120 donors gave £134 million via payroll giving, the tax relief on which was £40 million (www.gov.uk).

Is it worth exploring?

Yes, simply by offering it to any donor as one of the ways of supporting your charity. However, specifically targeting payroll gifts will often be worthwhile only if you can get access to a particular workforce and make a direct appeal to them – and this is a big 'if'. As there are many thousands of charities, companies can't realistically agree to let them all in, but you may have some special connection that can get them to open the door and, indeed, to support your appeal themselves. Local hospices, for example, might have a strong case with local employers – after all, they and their staff may well become beneficiaries of the hospice themselves in times to come. If you can get such privileged access, it is very well worth doing.

The costs of fundraising

How much does fundraising cost?

Generally speaking, it costs money to make money. Even the smallest charities and voluntary groups will incur some costs, whether it is the creation or mailing of materials, the costs of putting on an event, or the salaries of the members of staff involved in raising funds. The key thing to bear in mind is the balance between what you are spending, and what you are bringing in.

Occasionally debate about fundraising costs flares up usually as a result of a particular charity failing to adequately explain what it does and someone taking a view that costs are inherently bad things. The Institute of Fundraising's guidance that is designed to support the Code of Fundraising Practice states:

> *Calculations relating to fundraising costs or cost ratios are not a measure of the effectiveness of a charity. It is unfair to compare the costs or cost ratios of one organisation with another because of differences in activities and therefore, the way organisations account*

for costs. It is advisable for all charities to take opportunities to explain that fundraising is an investment which requires resources up front.

IoF n.d.a

How much is it right to spend on fundraising?

It will depend entirely on the circumstances of your organisation, what you are trying to achieve, and how you think best to go about it. In some cases, where the need is great and no one else is there to meet it, there might be little dispute about whether substantial costs are justified.

There are other cases where it can look as if a charity is attempting to expand beyond what its natural constituency* can provide at a reasonable cost. If you find that every further pound you spend is struggling to bring in a fair return, perhaps the time has come to think again. To get a feel for how your organisation's return on investment compares with others, look at the accounts of charities doing similar work to your own (they can be found on the register of charities at www.gov.uk/government/organisations/charity-commission).

There are no clear rights or wrongs; just do what you think is right and explain both what you have done and why you have done it in your annual reports. But professional fundraising does work. Spend the money, with reasonable intelligence, and the rewards will normally come in.

The point about explaining what you have spent, and why, is one that is becoming increasingly important. Many charities present their fundraising costs poorly in their annual reports, or simply don't mention them at all, no doubt for fear of frightening their supporters or feeling pressure to demonstrate that the highest proportion of funds is going to 'the front line'. The fact is that administration costs, what it takes to run a charity effectively, are crucial. A care worker providing support in a hospice is of reduced usefulness if there is no electricity or water because the bills haven't been paid. If you feel you can't justify the cost of your fundraising activities to your donors, you should be reviewing them as a matter of urgency.

✱ Constituency: as in political areas

2 Starting fundraising

Your fundraising strategy

You have to do three things. Together they make up what is called your fundraising strategy.

1 Decide who is going to give you money

Unless your charity is large and well known and will attract donations on reputation alone, you need names, or groups from which you will be able to get names, rather than generalisations like 'people in our town', or 'local businesses'. It is specific requests to individuals that you want to be able to make. Even if you are looking to raise money from companies or other organisations, it is the individuals responsible for making the decisions who you need to convince, not the organisation.

2 Make sure these people know and like you and what you do

Not much money is given to strangers. No matter how convincing your request, it is a weak start if the potential donor is actually thinking, 'who on earth are these people?'

3 Ask them, repeatedly, for money

Much of the most productive fundraising is in the form of face-to-face or at least telephone requests. There are all sorts of ways of arranging for such requests to be made – at your events, ringing people you know, or using a personal referral ('so and so suggested I contact you'), indeed on every occasion you or your colleagues meet other people. Personal letters, and to a greater extent circular mailings, rate second best. Other forms of advertising are likely to generate smaller returns, but they can produce new leads to be approached more productively. If you do go down the route of a less personal request for funds, it can often be helpful to soften the approach by offering some modest inducement, such as a raffle or lottery ticket, or entry into a draw.

Who to ask for money

Every charity is different and there is no simple answer. It will depend largely on the answers to the following questions.

Who is most likely to feel an interest in what we do?

This is your fundraising 'constituency' (though you may have a number of them). For example, the starting point for a charity like the Dystonia Society is likely to be people and families who have been affected by this medical condition; the Falkirk Local History Society will probably be looking to civically minded citizens, probably a different though overlapping group to those who support the Falkirk Youth Theatre. The Karuna Trust, seeking support for Buddhist development projects in India, simply targets households in reasonably prosperous areas of any city, but this is much more challenging.

What resources do we have?

Your main initial resource is likely to be people. Look at yourselves. Your first need may be to recruit others to join your group. If you have determined and confident trustees, you may be able to raise money highly effectively by straightforward personal requests, as Joan Brander did for the Winged Fellowship, described in the following case study. Or you may have people with experience and expertise in organising big fundraising events. You may have investors willing to finance the development of your fundraising. Or you may just be starting out as a small group of people on your own, with no resources and few contacts. This is how most great fundraising charities started. They learned and grew by doing it.

Case study: from charismatic funder to professional fundraising

Without the drive and determination of charismatic founders, many charities would simply not be around today. Joan Brander was one such person. In the 1960s she was involved with a WRVS-inspired holidays scheme for disabled people. After hearing Joan's constant reflections on the inadequacy of services, her husband said, 'Do something about it please!'

Joan became the founding trustee of the Winged Fellowship Trust, which continues to today as Revitalise. She inspired people to donate cash, materials and labour, and the first Winged Fellowship holiday centre was born. Like most good ideas, it began to grow. Other centres emerged, led by local converts. Joan led the team by example, giving vast amounts of time.

The unpaid, committed, local pioneers complemented the drive, enthusiasm and belief systems of the founding trustee. The staff agenda became a mix of the cause and a burning need to do more, regardless of resources, because that was the example being set.

Autonomy grew and although the organisation provided broadly the same service at each location, local rules applied. The committed needed the autonomy to get things done. This approach served the organisation well for quite some time. There seemed to be a global but unwritten mission statement. Unwritten, it was nevertheless in Technicolor.

As the concept grew, more paid staff were recruited. Centres had to be professionally managed. Marketing became a requirement. As the need for more money arose, central office employed professional fundraisers to supplement a wealth of local fundraisers, often charismatic individuals themselves, recruited by Joan, who had an eye for spotting the talented, the caring and the committed.

By the mid-1990s Joan was no longer a trustee but she remained involved, having a personal manual database of long-standing committed donors. Joan would keep meticulous records of the hundreds of people she corresponded with. She knew when the son or daughter of a donor had a birthday; she always sent them a birthday card. But professionalisation was also required. Donors needed upgrading and staff required boundaries. No one person could replace Joan; it had to be the task of many in a complex and challenging environment.

The past five years have been filled with growing pains, though to change too quickly would destroy that innate passion injected by the founding trustee. Staff, both existing managers and rising stars, needed to be shown new ways of working to gain a more corporate sense and they began to work to collective standards. Clearer guidelines for local supporters were drawn up. For example, it's OK to have a local bank account but you must go through the charity to open an account in its name, provide returns and not disturb the organisation's revenue streams while still purchasing what the organisation needs.

On the way there were casualties. Some could not work in such an environment. 'Are we losing our spontaneity?' was a common cry, but overall the passion and commitment laid down by Joan Brander is a lasting legacy today.

Pat Wallace 2003

Do we need 'good' money or will 'not so good' money do?

This may seem a silly question but it is not. For most charities there is good money and not so good money. Good money has two characteristics:
- it is free for you to spend as you think best (general donations);
- it has the potential to be ongoing, year after year (regular, committed donors, or replicable fundraising events, say).

Not so good money:
- is for one specified purpose only (so-called restricted funds);
- is short term rather than renewable (one-off or project grants).

There is often a mismatch in the availability of the two kinds of money. The not-so-good, short-term project grants can be relatively easy to get, while the regular ongoing funding is as hard work as it ever was. This has tempted many charities into over-expansion on the basis of short-term grant funding. Then, after a few happy years, such funders move on, and the charity is left hanging in the air. The people who give these grants, usually government (local or national), the Lottery or grant-making trusts and foundations, are sometimes accused of 'funding to fail'. Few of them will support your charity's efforts to develop a sustainable flow of fundraised income.

Getting known

How do we get future funders to know and like us, and what we do?

This depends entirely on who you have decided to raise your money from. The key is to have a planned (and budgeted) programme to make your charity well known to these people.

Different target groups will need quite different approaches. As one example, think about the following strategy for those seeking grants from local authorities:

Developing or keeping grant support from a local authority

Start out with a clear idea of what you want and how you are going to get it:
- Decide on a budget – perhaps 2.5% of the intended grant?
- Identify all those in the authority who might have some influence on how your work is seen – perhaps about 100 names of councillors and officers from a number of departments, including the treasurer's and the PR people's, and prepare address labels for all of them.
- Set up a programme for each of these people to receive or see something positive about your charity at least once a month – invitations, newsletters, press cuttings, Christmas cards or whatever (cheap to do in local authorities which will distribute materials internally free of charge).
- Towards the decision date for the grant, begin a programme to lobby the key players, informally or formally – a drink in the pub with your chair may be just as good as a formal meeting in the civic offices.

In other situations, use other methods. The box below has two more quite different, but real examples from Luke FitzHerbert's experience of small new charities putting themselves on the map for those on whose future support they would rely.

Case study: the Brent River Society

This was (and is) wholly local, and seeks support from environmentally concerned citizens. 'Events' were an important means of getting publicity, the biggest of which was called the Grand Opening of the Brent River Park. The local authority had offered to contribute some hundreds of pounds to our project. The Society persuaded them to use it to buy the oak for about 30 new footpath signposts to be constructed and carved by local secondary schools. They were then unveiled by the Mayor in a four-mile procession, led by a volunteer pipe band and followed by a large crowd. The Society must have reached thousands for minimal expenditure by the local authority, and none by itself.

The National Pyramid Trust

This was quite different. It was set up to establish preventive volunteer-led therapy groups for primary schoolchildren at risk of educational failure. The plan was for the groups, once established, to be funded out of local educational budgets but to seek funding from trusts and foundations for the development work of getting these local schemes set up.

Once the relevant trusts had been identified, the people concerned, along with senior people involved with such issues from universities and government departments – the 'stakeholders', to use the jargon – were invited to a briefing, followed by lunch, just 'to discuss with us our plans for taking the work forward'. The event had credibility because it was hosted for the charity by a foundation, the Gulbenkian. Though not itself big enough to become a major funder, Gulbenkian was and is recognised as expert in this kind of work.

No money was asked for at the meeting, but many hundreds of thousands of pounds followed in due course from the trusts that had got to hear of Pyramid at that early stage – even those who did not come to the briefing – (and, eventually, the ongoing funding for all the pilot projects was indeed generated from local sources).

Luke FitzHerbert 2003

Your case for funding

Why should people give us their money?

Before you start asking your target people for money, you should be clear about your 'case'. This is not so much because you will meet with many difficult questions but because unless you yourselves are clear and confident about your case, you will not come across convincingly to others.

This case will have two different parts:

- First, you will show that there is a real, urgent and important need for what you do or are proposing to do.

- Second, you will show that yours is a well-organised and impressive organisation which they can trust to use their money well.

In the fundraising courses run by DSC, we use the checklist of possible selling points, set out in the following box. Most charities should be able to point to about eight of the ten.

What are your main selling points?

About your work

- **The urgency or the extent of the problem of need**
  If you don't think it is really important, why should anyone else? But it does not have to be more important than other causes – we need both ballet and an end to child cruelty.

- **Its emotional or sympathetic appeal**
  Donations are more about liking than thinking, so this is usually essential. It is therefore hard to get donations for charities that are away from the front line, like national associations, or CVSs (but they may have particular projects with greater appeal).

- **Its innovations**
  Charity is always with us, but any convincing new approach, or just a new element in an existing approach, is attractive.

- **Its cost-effectiveness**
  Can you offer a lot in return for the money, perhaps through the involvement of volunteers? If so, make the point. If not, focus on your other selling points.

- **Its value as an investment for the future**
  Will their donation live on doing good for years, or will you just be back for more for the same need for the same people next year?

- **The unhappy consequences if your work were to stop**
  Be careful that this does not come across as a whine. 'The children will starve and it will be your fault' is not a successful approach.

About your organisation

- **Its appearance of excellence**
  Everything about you, from your telephone manner to your letterhead and your annual report should be better than expected for a charity of your kind – and all this without looking expensive either! This means hard work, and money, but you should be able to get a small grant for this if you need it (see page 80)

- **Its independent endorsements**
  If you are wonderful, as all DSC readers' organisations are, you will be able to get endorsements from people known to the donors, at least by reputation, and with no axe to grind, who will say 'these people are really pretty good'.

- **Its record of previous successes**
  'Success breeds success' and 'to them that hath shall more be given'. If you have had successes, make sure they show. If not, can you quote the successes of others whose lead you are following?

- **The strength of its voluntary input**
  Most donors like the 'voluntary' part of the voluntary sector. All charities have volunteers (its trustees, if no others) so have them up front when fundraising – it's where they belong.
- **Its community support**
  Are you one of those single-minded, almost crazed fanatics who has been solely responsible for building up most of our greatest charities? Good for you if you are, but hide it for fundraising purposes as it can deter donors who prefer to see that you are able to work with lots of different organisations and have a wide range of support from your local community.

How do we get across the need for our work?

The basic appeal is best if it is simple:

'People with this condition need help and support and they are not getting it.'

'Because of us, children living on the street in Brazil get proper lives.'

'Our town looks a mess. Let's sort it out.'

'There are people here, caring full time for family members, who never get a holiday or a break.'

'Everyone deserves the chance of a decent and dignified death.'

'We must nurture a new generation of young musicians.'

'Help lonely old people get together at our weekly lunch clubs.'

... and then?

1 Don't give more detail, give examples instead. Donors give money when they are moved far more often than when they are convinced. And what moves people is the particular example, far more than the persuasive argument. See the box below for a good example from Oxfam. And remember that, if you can't talk to the donor personally, then a picture is indeed worth a thousand words.

2 Say, very briefly, how you organise the work – we fund researchers, organise volunteer respite carers, or whatever. Only elaborate if asked. Donors tend to be much more interested in the people or situation that you are addressing than in the mechanics of how you do it.

Caution!

Some people get very worked up about language. You may have noticed that in this book I occasionally use words like 'old' rather than 'elderly', and so on. The language you use is really important, and it's sometimes necessary to steer a middle course between the language that we prefer within our own organisations and that which donors use in their daily lives. To insist on using our professional phraseology, even when it will serve to put off the very people who we are seeking to recruit to the cause, can seem as patronising as the other way round. Nevertheless, it is one thing for a group of older people to choose to call themselves 'old', and another for a twentysomething-year-old to label people 'old'.

We all use jargon when it is useful internally or when dealing with others in our field, but we can avoid it when talking – let alone writing – to donors. 'Outreach', 'BME', 'ESF', 'outcome-based', 'key stage' and 'service provision' and 'service users' are typically common words and phrases that most 'normal' people will not connect with in the same way that you or your colleagues do. Even apparently commonplace words or phrases like 'beneficiaries', 'line management', 'housing benefit', 'therapy', 'human resources' or 'advocacy' are best either avoided or explained.

Example: Oxfam

Oxfam, with an income of over £300 million a year, does almost every kind of work in almost all parts of the world. How do you put this in less than 300 words? This is the text of one of their general purpose fundraising pages at www.oxfam.org.uk (half the space on the page is taken up by a picture of Amna, the girl described).

It is important to get an education. I want to come to school so that I will be able to teach other young girls so they will have better lives' Amna Khatoon Brohi, schoolgirl (and future teacher), Sindh, Pakistan

When nine-year old Amna's school was swept away by devastating floods in 2010, she thought her dreams of one day becoming a teacher were over. But with a little help from Oxfam supporters, her dream is back on track.

Like many girls in Pakistan, Amna faced an uphill battle to get an education. Outdated teaching methods, lack of equipment, early marriage, and attitudes to girls' schooling mean that in rural areas like Sindh, only one in three women have ever attended school. Amna knew that without an education it would be hard to escape the poverty that she – and her parents before her – grew up in. We wanted to help kick-start a change.

It doesn't take a lot to help Amna and other girls get an education that can change their lives – for good. We're helping communities to build 'model schools' that can withstand floods and have proper sanitation facilities so parents know their daughters' dignity and privacy will be respected. We're training teachers to make lessons more engaging and raise standards in the classroom. And we're working to inspire communities to value education for all their children, girls as well as boys.

Reproduced in shortened format courtesy of Oxfam GB

What about reasoned argument?

It has its place, but its use in fundraising is often indirect. The best way to demonstrate your credibility, when fundraising, is not by argument but by endorsement. Use your arguments to persuade the right people to endorse your work (the right people are those who enjoy the respect or affection of your potential donors).

For example, a personal recommendation by Bob Geldof, based on personal knowledge of its work, might be extremely valuable to a small overseas aid charity; so might the endorsement by the local football club manager for your scheme for a new youth club; or by the lord lieutenant of the county for your town festival; or by the chair of the county law society for your new legal advice idea. In all cases, the people concerned will be putting their own reputations on the line, so they will need to be convinced of the good sense of your project.

Many organisations benefit greatly from the endorsement and support of celebrities. Just look at the example of Princess Diana and land mines. But media celebrity can backfire; and you should not have to pay.

Caution!

For fundraising purposes, it is usually unproductive to try to persuade people who are not on your side already. For example, if someone assumes that most asylum seekers are scroungers, just ask someone else less prejudiced. There are nearly always plenty of well-disposed people out there only too happy to support you if they are asked. You may well want to convert the sceptical for all sorts of other excellent reasons, but don't expect it to raise much money.

The most unlikely causes find supporters, although depending on the cause you are trying to raise money for, it may be more or less difficult to attract them. However, if what you are trying to do is important to you and you can articulate it with passion, there will almost certainly be others who can be convinced to support you.

You may be looking for funding to put on a niche art installation, for example, or raising funds in aid of a rare medical need, which by virtue of its rarity has a connection with fewer people than more 'popular' causes. In such cases you may have to work a bit harder to identify your fundraising constituency, but once you have found them, you may find that your request for help resonates that much more with them.

What makes a strong case for funding?

You need to be able to give clear, consistent and uncomplicated answers, at a range of levels, to the question 'why do you need my money?' Many potential funders will only want to talk at one of these levels, but you must be prepared to meet them at the level they choose, which could include:

- your vision and mission – why you exist;
- your long-term goals;
- your immediate objectives;
- your financial needs.

The following box gives an example.

Example: Blankshire Children's Society

Vision and mission

Children brought up in care have poor life prospects, often because they have missed out on their education and so have low levels of literacy.

This is largely avoidable. These children deserve as good an education as other children, but they often don't get it, usually through no fault whatsoever of their own. We exist to change this situation.

Goals

We want every child in care in Blankshire to have the same level of personal support for their education that we would expect for our own children.

Second, we want the county council to take the issue far more seriously. At present they have no idea how these children are doing at school.

Immediate objectives

First we intend every child to have a permanent, voluntary adult mentor for their education, who will stay with them as they move from foster home to foster home. Through their mentor they will have the same consistent encouragement and support, in both term time and holidays, as other children.

Second, we will persuade the county council to keep and publish figures on the educational progress of the children in its care, so that this can be monitored and action taken where necessary.

Financial needs

The mentor programme

We need to support 18 existing mentors supporting 48 children this year and we intend to recruit, train and have in place six more mentors.

The annual cost of the existing service is £24,000, or £750 a child, funded by the donations of our supporters. The support of six new mentors will mean a further £8,000 a year is needed (their recruitment and training will be funded by grants from foundations).

The campaigning programme, to influence the county council, is carried out by our voluntary committee members but we have budgeted £4,000 to give them the office support they need.

A copy of the detailed budgets is available on request.

How do we fundraise for core costs: salaries or administrative and overhead costs?

Raising money for things like this is not easy. Fortunately, it is also not necessary.

The general rule is to raise money for what you do, not for the costs of doing it. Almost all charities are doing work that is attractive to donors, providing it is brought to their attention. Donors are, generally speaking, not interested in any breakdown of the costs in doing so. If it costs you £10,000 every year to bring 15 sick children from Chernobyl for a holiday in Britain, they will decide that this is good value, or not, without usually being interested in how much of it is salaries, how much air fares and so on. After all, when you buy a loaf of bread, do you worry about the administration costs of the shop, or the levels of staff salaries in the bakery? You are only interested in what you get for your money. So it is with most donors.

However, there are some donors who will be interested, and on occasion debate on charity administration costs flares up in the media, prompting questions from donors about costs. This is where it pays to be prepared, and as transparent as possible. The relationship between your costs and your income should be clear from your annual report and accounts, and I would say that is the place for it, rather than as additional, unnecessary detail in your fundraising materials. It is common for questions about administration costs to be sparked by simple misunderstandings about how a charity works, or what it may be doing at a specific point in time.

Grant-making charities will certainly be interested in your budgets, but this is usually just to satisfy themselves that you are properly organised and are therefore likely to achieve what you have promised to achieve – which is what they are funding. The people who really are obsessed with the details of your costs are local authorities and other public bodies, whose excessive attention to such issues derives from historical concerns about the misuse of public money. There is a certain irony in the way that these funders actually increase the administrative costs of the work being funded, through their often onerous and superfluous application processes and reporting requirements.

But money for salaries or administration is what we actually need!

Are you sure? Often a more useful way to look at it is that the money isn't needed for your organisation, but for the work that you do. You do not have to say 'in order to pay my salary, please give me £20,000' when you could say 'in order for these unfortunate children to have their holiday, please give me £20,000'. This is not trickery. It is actually the accurate and proper approach. Look at the following example, showing two ways of presenting the same costs (for a fictitious, simplified community centre).

Example: core costs and overheads

Worton Community Centre

A 2015 Costs

Salaries	£30,000
Rent	£8,000
Office costs, telephone etc.	£6,000
Repairs and renovations	£6,000
Total	**£50,000**

B 2015 Costs

Drop-in centre	£8,000
Lunch clubs	£14,000
Youth club	£18,000
Holiday programme	£10,000
Total	**£50,000**

Note that both lists are recording the same money. The first list shows what the money was spent on, the second shows what it was spent for. (Note also that the second way of putting it, not the first, is the one expected by the Charity Commission in a charity's accounts, with the first being just an optional extra for the 'Notes').

Is it easier to ask for money for the things in List A or in List B? The answer is obvious, but we still find charity after charity asking for money for the rent or the phone bill or the salary or whatever when they could be raising it for the old or young people who need their club. You're not hiding anything by presenting what you need in this way (and you'll need to know the individual costs anyway), but showing donors and funders what their money will actually do, rather than the detail of what it will be spent on, is a much more powerful message. It's useful to remember that funders are people too, and they often care about your cause at least as much as you do. Organising your costs in a way that reinforces what you are going to do is far more likely to get them excited about supporting you than the prospect of paying your rent and telephone bill.

What if our work doesn't break down into easy bits?

There are many ways of breaking down the costs of your work that do not involve headings like salaries or rent. Here are some examples, where the salaries and so on simply do not appear.

- **The cost per activity:** as in the example above: 'The youth club in our centre costs £18,000 a year'.
- **The cost per beneficiary:** your total costs divided by the number of people you help: 'Our training programme costs £250 for each trainee'.
- **Cost per location:** your total costs divided among the areas where you work: 'Our service in Alloa costs £2,000 a year, in Falkirk £3,000'.
- **Cost per event:** ideal for many arts groups: 'Our performance of *Hamlet* in Cardiff prison in January will cost £4,000, of *As you Like It* in Belmarsh in June, £3,000.
- **Cost per day, week or month:** your total costs divided by 365, 52 or 12. We can all do this: 'We need 52 sponsors for our Keep Doncaster Clean programme'.
- **Cost per achievement:** your total cost divided by the number of successes achieved: 'It costs £30 to get each child through its bicycling test'.

What if someone wants to know about our salaries, rent and so on?

You have nothing to hide, so just tell them, but these are unlikely to be the most important things they need to know. When approaching a possible donor, concentrate on saying what could be achieved with their money and what benefits their money would bring; everything else is secondary and subsidiary.

Is this the 'outcome funding' approach?

Yes, and the various Lottery distributors, most government programmes, a number of grant-making trusts all focus on outcomes as the main determining factor in whether they will award funds or not. Outcomes are often contrasted with outputs. If 20 young people complete your mentoring programme, that's a measure of output: 20 people went through and came out the other end. But the outcomes might be quite different. What difference did it make to those young people's lives? What skills do they have now and how are they applying them?

In many ways, this is an easier way to communicate to potential funders or donors. You can be passionate and engaging around the specific changes you are trying to make in the world in a way that is hard to do if you only focus on the activity you are using to make it happen. Contrast 'we want to train 20 young people in key skills that will help them to get a job' (output) with 'we want to change the lives of 20 young people by increasing their confidence and getting them into work' (outcomes).

This approach is not without its challenges, however. Depending on what you are trying to achieve you may need to think very hard about what the outcomes of your work or project will be, and how you will measure them. If one of the outcomes is increased confidence, how do you measure that? Can you create or use a questionnaire with the young people before and after your work with them to show the progress they've made and demonstrate the outcome you are looking for? In terms of getting them into work, that is an easy measure in one way, but separating the impact of your work from any other factors may be difficult.

The most important thing is to see this as being a part of your work, not a part of your fundraising. If you are planning what you want to achieve and are interested in how effective it is (which you should be), working that into your request for funding is easy.

Some danger signs that funders look out for

Experienced funders are often on the lookout for some of the more common potential danger signs:

- an organisation which does not give the impression of being in control financially;
- an organisation which is run by its staff with the trustees effectively sidelined;
- an organisation where the fundraising applicant seems separated and distant from the work being done;
- people raising money for their own activities that are not fully integrated into the rest of the organisation's work.

Isn't more detail needed for grant applications?

For applications for small amounts (say up to £1,000 or £2,000) to small grant-makers, and unless their guidelines say otherwise, a simple request for £x with which to achieve your results is usually enough (when accompanied by a decent annual report and accounts).

For big grants you will often need to put in a more formal funding application, perhaps even with business plans and so on. Many trusts or foundations making such grants specify in some detail what they want (see 'Applying for grants' on page 73.)

But a full, formal funding application for smaller projects can actually put off many donors, even institutional ones, who just want to support a good cause when they are asked nicely and with feeling. They may well feel irritated by being treated as an office with procedures and requirements when they want to think of themselves simply as concerned and benevolent individuals. Send only what they ask for; you can always say you have the full 42-page business plan if they want it.

Example: making your case

Here is an example of an exercise that has previously been used on our Effective Fundraising training course.

Suppose that you have had the following letter:

> My mother has recently died and in her will she asked me to give £10,000 to a charity of my choice. I am asking four organisations, of which yours is one, to give me a ring and say what you could do with a gift like this.

Prepare your call in reply to this. I suggest a one-minute maximum to start with – quite a long time on the phone.

The following examples (from the fictitious Age Support charity in Blankshire) show two ways of approaching this, with most people's starting effort being something very like A:

Response A

I am ringing from Age Support in response to your letter. Is this a convenient time to speak?

First, Age Support is very sorry to hear of your mother's death. Please accept the charity's condolences.

You ask about our work. Age Support in Blankshire was founded in 1937. In the first 30 years we concentrated on our volunteer driver scheme to help people who had not got, or couldn't use transport of their own, and indeed this is still running. Now, we support elderly people and their carers throughout the area in many different ways and we have grown until we have 27 professional staff on a range of projects – as well as lots of volunteers. Our services range from day centres and lunch clubs to advice surgeries and referral schemes. We also have a big outreach project as well as running a money advice clinic.

We are partly funded by the local authority, and a few of the projects bring in some of their own income, but we are always short of money and your mother's £10,000 would be an enormous boost and would of course be recognised in our next annual report.

I hope you will agree that this would make really good use of your mother's legacy.

This is more about your organisation than about your beneficiaries. It is also dry and impersonal, partly in the third person rather than the first, and uses jargon words like 'referral' and 'outreach'. Compare it with the following.

Response B

I am ringing from Age Support in Blankshire in response to your lovely letter. Is this a good time for us to talk?

First, I am very sorry to hear of your mother's death. Please accept our condolences. Did she know us?

So, what could we achieve with £10,000? Can I give you a couple of examples? Take our money advice scheme, because many elderly people are driven mad trying to cope with housing benefit and so on. Just yesterday, for example, Mrs Smith, who is housebound, told us she thought she was going to be evicted because her housing benefit claim was 'invalid', but she couldn't find out what was wrong with it because they just never called her back. Quite easy for us to clear up but a desperate worry for her – and she's 87! This whole service costs us less than £20,000 a year to run so your mum's £10,000 would help a whole lot for people like her!

Or would she have been more interested in our lunch clubs and drop-in centres? Loneliness is awful when you are old and we can do a great deal about it. And it's not expensive as they are mainly run by the old people themselves.

But may I ask you, what do you think your mother would have been most interested in?

This is much better, though my own preference would be neither of the above, just 'We do all sorts. Can you tell me what your mum was interested in and why you put us on your list?' Then you can go on to tailor your suggestion to their mother's/their own interests.

How do we show that our organisation is first class of its kind?

Here are some ideas.

1 You will be judged by appearances so it is a very great help to have printed materials that are seriously impressive for the kind of organisation you are (without them looking expensive). Check:

   – The design of your letterhead and the quality of the paper: photocopy quality is not usually good enough.

   – The appearance and style of your letters: they should have wide margins, no spelling mistakes or other careless errors, simple clear English, and should sound like a letter from a charity not a business.

   – Your leaflets and newsletters: do not try to save money by amateur design, and do not have too many words. Keep them short, simple and strong. Longer is usually worse, in fundraising terms. Often the pictures are central with only a very few words needed to explain them – and a few big pictures are far better than lots of small ones.

– Your annual report and accounts: is this a document of powerful conviction or just a few printed pages pinned together?

And if all this seems too expensive, get a small grant specifically to enable you to present yourselves properly in public. There is a list of sources of small grants on the DSC website (www.dsc.org.uk).

2 Obtain short endorsement letters from people who are independent of your organisation and with no axe to grind, saying how good you are (I assume that you are pretty good, of your kind).

3 Ensure that everyone fundraising for your organisation is fully briefed and obviously committed to the work of the charity.

3 Getting donations from individuals

The most recent figures suggest that nearly £9 billion was given to charities by individuals in 2012 (Dobbs et al. 2012). Of this, 40% was in gifts of £100 or more. Most of this is 'good' money: given for the work of the charity as a whole. A quarter or so comes in legacies and about another quarter is the very best money of all – regular donations or subscriptions, usually by bankers order or direct debit and set to continue until further notice.

Basic principles

What are the stages in raising money from individual donors?

1   **Acquisition:** getting the first donation, hopefully with the means of contacting donors again.
2   **Retention:** keeping them as regular or at least occasional donors.
3   **Development:** encouraging them to give more, or more often.

In practical terms the three stages come in this order, but in financial terms it is usually the other way round – more money will usually come from going back to existing supporters or contacts than from finding new ones. It is a common mistake for established charities to neglect those they already have in favour of an all-consuming search for new donors.

How can donors be approached?

Most fundraising charities use a combination of:

- direct mail;
- sponsored activities;
- fundraising events;
- door-to-door collections;
- lotteries, raffles, games;
- personal solicitation (just asking).

Just asking, whether face-to-face or on the telephone, is probably the most important in financial terms for very many charities, but it is also a bit alarming for many people starting on fundraising, so we will leave it for the moment and come back to it later. But don't forget, if you need money, the easiest, quickest way to get it is to ask for it directly. (I don't count writing a letter as 'asking' in this context.) The following box shows how different approaches can be combined, and can develop over time.

Case study: St Luke's Hospice Plymouth

St Luke's Hospice is in Plymouth, a former dockyard city with not much tradition of philanthropy, but a strong sense of community. It was founded by a group of people, none of them particularly well off, centred on a church in the city centre. It took this group five years of personal community fundraising of every kind to be able to buy their first house – with seven bedrooms all upstairs and no lift. When the hospice opened, the freshly recruited medical staff were warned that first, they would all have to do a bit of everything – fundraising as well as washing up – and second, they only had enough money to pay the wages for three weeks!

Now, more than 30 years later, St Luke's has a purpose-built building and a staff of 300 and over 1,000 volunteers, many of whom still contribute to the fundraising, though there is now a substantial and professional fundraising team as well.

A recent fundraising idea that has proven very successful for the hospice was inspired by the 2014 poppy display in London, which marked 100 years since the first full day of Britain's involvement in the First World War. For the Forget-Me-Not appeal, the hospice planted more than 1,000 handcrafted plastic forget-me-not flowers, created by Theatre Royal Plymouth, in a seafront garden, giving the local community the chance to remember a loved one in a unique way. The event was launched with a floral flourish by journalist and television presenter, Angela Rippon.

The interesting aspect of this type of event is that people are not, at least on the surface, giving donations at all: they are buying a forget-me-not for £25 to celebrate the life of someone they love. This event generated more than £55,000 in just one month and is being adopted as a fundraising idea by many other hospices up and down the country, with St Luke's acting as an agent to facilitate this.

With this method of contributing to a local hospice, and similarly (although quite differently in approach) with St Luke's Lottery where you have the chance to win £1,000, £200, or £10 every week, relatively few people see themselves as 'donors'. Those who give larger amounts than the recommended £25 (or £1 in the case of the Lottery) often see this more as an appropriate contribution for the services provided by St Luke's – or, perhaps, for services to be provided in the future. It is all wholly dependent on the hospice being accepted as the community asset it is.

A mainstay of St Luke's fundraising efforts is getting people involved in its many events and challenges. The charity's website encourages individuals to fundraise by taking part in various challenges, from an overseas cycling challenge in Costa Rica to trekking in the Sahara, and events, from coffee mornings to tandem skydives. The charity provides an easy way to register for these events and challenges and has several online giving pages and ways to support individual fundraisers, including stlukes-hospice.org.uk/donate, which includes instructions of how to donate by text message. An example of an event in 2015, with the funds raised via St Luke's JustGiving web page, was of a group of friends, Denise, Tone, Bev and Mark who ran the Plymouth Half Marathon. They raised £2,001.93 for the hospice in memory of Roz Greening: 'a keen runner, an inspirational and amazing mother and wife, and treasured friend to many', who spent her final days supported by hospice staff at St Luke's.

Direct mail

What is direct mail?

This is the term used for sending fundraising letters by post to people listed on your donor base. Though the letter may be a one-off appeal, each mailing is usually part of a regular organised mailing programme. You and your colleagues will undoubtedly receive an array of fundraising mail through the letterbox at home. It can be a useful exercise to collect any mailings received over a number of weeks and then get together to discuss them. What works and doesn't work? Doing this can help you to discover which approach would suit your organisation best.

How do we get a donor base?

You probably have one already, even if it only has the small number of people involved in setting up your organisation. You then build on this by every means possible; namely by:

- asking everyone you meet if they would like to be kept in touch with what you do;
- asking people for the names of other people you might write to;
- collecting names and addresses at your events;
- generating publicity that prompts people to approach you;
- swapping lists with other organisations (called reciprocal mailings and generally a good thing to do);
- buying lists, which is trickier.

How many people might we have on our donor base?

It varies from charity to charity. But it is as easy to have too many as too few. And if you invest one year on expanding your database, you must be willing to be quite ruthless in cutting it back again if the money is not coming in.

Is it alright to put our clients or their families on our mailing list?

Sure, unless there are some very special circumstances. If they themselves are unlikely to have the resources to be significant donors, you can ask if they have relatives or friends who might be happy to support you.

Won't we need more than one list?

You will probably quickly find that you need to 'code' your list because different people will need to get different letters (this is called segmentation). A starting division might be:

- **the hot list:** these are your active supporters and donors;
- **a warm list:** for those who in some way show interest in what you do: 'Thanks for coming to our bring and buy sale yesterday. Can we interest you further …?';
- **cold lists:** for people who don't yet know you: 'As a local resident, can I interest you in …?

How do we manage our lists?

A perfectly adequate database comes as part of the package with most computers. It will keep all the information you need and print out labels for you. You will need to keep, as a minimum, for each person:

- name and address;
- the date and amount of all donations;
- space for notes.

Very soon, if not immediately, you will find yourself also wanting:

- telephone numbers;
- email addresses;
- the date and nature of previous mailings/contacts.

DSC (publishers of this book) also publishes *The Complete Customer Relationship Management Handbook,* which is packed with advice on setting up and using databases to manage your contacts (details at www.dsc.org.uk/crm). For larger charities, there are specialised donor-base packages available. If you think that you may need something more advanced than a simple database, the Institute of Fundraising has a range of software providers listed on their website (www.institute-of-fundraising.org.uk).

How do we keep our lists up to date?

By unremitting hard work. We all get annoyed by inaccurate and out-of-date mailings. So you have to work out and continually review exactly how you are going to keep yours accurate.

Furthermore it is not just accuracy but also good management that is needed. You probably have a few very important supporters, for example. How are you going to make sure that they do not get the same letters as the person who has given you £5? Managing your donor base calls for continuous intelligent effort – it is not a mere administrative routine to be delegated to whoever you can find.

In charities with a donor base of any size I would suggest giving one trustee the responsibility for keeping an eye on the quality of your mailing lists on behalf of the trustees as a whole. It is that important.

Should we have a membership or friends scheme?

Some charities are set up as membership organisations in the first place; others choose to introduce some kind of membership scheme. These may be useful, but one word of warning. For some people, a membership subscription carries an image of a much lower payment than that of a straight donation, and is often related to what you get back for it – like being a member of a golf club. This may not be appropriate for your situation.

There is nothing wrong with just having supporters.

Can we swap a mailing list with a similar organisation?

Yes, charities do this and it usually works. The total given to the combined charities will be more than the two get separately. Some people feel that their lists should be guarded with their lives, and never shared. This feeling generally comes from a misapprehension about your supporters. There are actually only a few who will just support you and will not support other similar organisations. And getting a letter from another organisation is not a reason to stop supporting you anyway.

Case study: the Brent River Society mailing list

This Society, wholly voluntary, was set up by myself, my wife and a small group of others to get the local authorities to create a linear park along four miles of the River Brent in west London. The idea grew out of one of the activities of a previously existing preservation society, so there was a core of a couple of dozen people already involved from the start. It was (and is) a membership organisation and the membership grew to almost 2,000 in just a few years, mainly through local publicity, centred on maps of the proposed park in the local paper and on public meetings. At these meetings everyone was asked from the platform to consider joining the Society and was then invited to do so personally at the door as they left.

A particular success was an invitation to sign a protest petition – the London County Council was proposing to put our nice river into a concrete trough. Everyone who signed also put their address – otherwise the signatures would carry no weight – and they were told that they would also be kept up to date with the outcome of the campaign. Hey presto! Several hundred new warm names on our mailing list.

Another interesting feature was (and is) the size of the subscription. Because campaigning was the first purpose of having the mailing list, with fundraising secondary, we wanted as many names as possible. We therefore set the subscription at '50p, or what you can afford'. Not only was no one deterred by the cost, but also many people were embarrassed to give so little – 50p obviously didn't cover even the cost of posting the newsletters three times a year. In practice our average subscription rapidly rose to over £5 a head – and this was nearly 30 years ago in a far from rich part of London.

Luke FitzHerbert 2003

What about data protection?

If you are using contact lists and databases to contact supporters, you will need to comply with data protection legislation. There are specific elements of legislation which will be more or less important depending on who you are contacting and what for, and these are laid out in the Institute of Fundraising's Code of Fundraising Practice. Their summary guidance is likely to be sufficient in most cases, for most organisations.

Data protection rules of thumb

The Institute of Fundraising's website provides the following practical advice:

Data protection legislation affects many areas of fundraising. Fundraisers need to ensure they comply with the regulations. These can be daunting but there are a few main things that you need to remember. It is most helpful to think about how you would like your details used by another organisation.

For example:

- *ensure you have the necessary permissions to contact supporters;*
- *do not retain any information on a supporter or prospect that you would not be comfortable sharing with them;*
- *do not use information in a manner that a supporter would not wish; and*
- *do not share data in a manner that a supporter would not wish.*

IoF n.d.b

What should we send in our mailings?

You should keep it as close as possible to a personal letter, and include the essential reply card or similar. This, if done well, will seldom be taken as junk mail. You may also include printed material as back-up. For very large organisations, it may be impossible to be convincingly personal, and other approaches may be needed, but that will not apply to most readers of this book.

Specifically:

- Your letter can actually be personal in many cases, not just appear to be so. One individual can probably 'top and tail' 100 letters in an hour – so three trustees could do 600 letters in an evening, with the date, salutation and signature all done by hand (and with some of them having a personal PS at the bottom).
- There must be a response mechanism. The easier it is for people to respond to your letter the better your results will be. The ideal letter will have a link to your website or online giving page, or a telephone number to ring with a credit card donation (hard for a small charity to arrange) and maybe also a card and envelope with as much as possible pre-printed. For example, including a standing order instruction where all the donor has to do is write in an amount and the name of their bank will get some donors who would otherwise not get round to finding their chequebook to donate. It is definitely worth considering using Freepost, the service from the Royal Mail which means the postage for any replies is paid by you, not the person posting it. You can register a Freepost address and set up an account at www.royalmail.com.
- Offering an opportunity to donate through your website can be the easiest way not only to get people to give, but also to present them with more information about your work than you could ever reasonably convey in a letter, especially images, case studies, video clips about your work, etc.

- You can enclose leaflets and so on, but they are inherently impersonal. If you do, try to connect them with your letter: 'I enclose a leaflet which has a nice picture of Mrs Smith on the inside', or whatever.

What should our letters say?

Almost anything can work if it is done nicely, but if you want some specific advice, try this:

1 The letter should say what a donation can do and should ask for the money to do it. '£10 a month can help us to give people with disabilities and their carers a proper holiday.' I think this is better than, 'Every year our supporters, and we hope you will become one of them, enable more than 150 people with severe disabilities, and their carers, to have a proper holiday'.

2 And then 'Can you send us a standing order – there is a pre-printed form on the back of this letter – or a cheque for whatever you can afford, in the attached envelope?' It is essential that your letter is absolutely clear about what you are asking for. There is nothing wrong with starting out 'Can you give us a donation of £x so that ...'.

3 You may offer an inducement. 'All subscribers will be offered two free tickets to our annual ball' (at which they will be invited to patronise the bar and buy tickets for the tombola) for example.

4 It is very important that if the person is already a supporter this is fully, accurately and properly recognised.

How long should the letter be?

This is up to you. What would you like to get yourself? There is a big difference between a letter and other enclosures. A letter is asking to be read through to the signature at the end. The attachments are for them to read in detail only if they want to. Try your letters out on people not connected with your charity. But unless it is genuinely interesting, a long letter is less likely to be read than a short one. Above all, you need a powerful message that will move the reader to action.

Should we ask for a specific amount?

If possible, yes, but this is difficult if you do not know what the recipient of your letter can afford. But if you give no guidance you may get £5 from someone who could have given you much more.

One approach is to give check boxes for a range of donations on the reply card: say £10, £25, £100, £250 and 'other amounts', or a monthly standing order for £2.50, £5, £10 or £25. You might want to link or match these to specific amounts and what you could do with them if you have mentioned in the main text of your letter. Be careful of putting amounts that are too small. Perhaps you could say that if the recipient cannot consider a substantial donation of the kind requested, they might help in another way, as a volunteer or by suggesting further names for your mailing list, or by writing in protest to the villain in your case.

What should we do with the responses?

One of the biggest mistakes you can make is not responding properly to the donations that you receive. Please ensure that within 48 hours you can, by post, phone or email:

- acknowledge receipt of the gift;
- thank the donor;
- cash the cheque (often forgotten, even when we have made a great fuss about how desperately the money is needed!).

You should also keep a record of when and how the above were done. This is where keeping a simple database can be extremely useful in keeping track of what contact has been had with which donors and helping to inform how and when you should follow up and contact them again.

How do we measure the success of our mailings?

You should record:

- the percentage response;
- the most frequent size of gift (i.e. the mode, which is more useful than the mean when it comes to averages);
- the percentage cost (money spent/money received, times 100);
- comments, while they are still fresh in your mind.

Little reports like this make good items for trustees' meetings, especially when they can be compared with previous mailings. These basic figures are essential if you are to measure the impact of changes to materials, mailing lists, or new approaches and make sure you are getting the best possible response.

Example: tone and style

For many years, I have kept the following example of a commercial direct mail consultant's circular letter – nothing to do with charity – showing a highly successful professional's approach to a completely cold mailing. When reading other people's draft charity fundraising letters, I try to imagine his comments on them. You might also like to compare this with the style of the trust application letter on page 77.

Oh no!
NOT <u>ANOTHER</u>
SALES LETTER

I suppose that as we are all expected to be Honest, Truthful and Legal these days, I had better come clean. The only excuse for this mailing is that every time I write a letter like this, business goes up by 25%.

Sounds too good to be true? Well, it must be added that it has taken 20 years of experience and about the same amount of time learning how to target mailings and to source lists.

I remember many years ago a pioneer of direct mail, long since gone to join the celestial postmaster in the sky, used to say to me: 'Keep it simple Mike – a brochure tells but a sales letter *SELLS!*' And he was absolutely right. Good direct mail can be amazingly simple, remarkably inexpensive and wonderfully effective. One of our clients *regularly* sells £1 million of his products using a two-colour sales letter we produced for him. The same letter ... over and over again ... *to the same lists*. Nothing is cheaper to produce, or harder working, than a good sales letter. After all, you are still reading this, aren't you?

Whatever the right approach may be – and if you need an all-singing and dancing, pop-up Day-Glo crashpack we can produce that too – we can create your mailing piece, supply the mailing list and mail it far cheaper and more effectively than you can do it yourself. <u>That's a promise.</u> In any area and any quantity and within the slimmest budgets.

Now that you are planning your autumn and Christmas campaigns, why not call me for some free advice on direct mail, design, copy and lists? Do it now and discover how to make direct mail work for you.

Michael Barford

Mike Barford

PS Act now and we'll show you how a silly PS like this can double your response!'

How often should we write?

The ideal answer is 'as often as the donor is happy to hear from you' – donors generally like hearing from the charities they support. If you acknowledge substantial donations with a thank-you telephone call (as well as the still obligatory immediate thank-you letter) this is an excellent opportunity to ask how often they are happy for you to write.

Otherwise the answer is usually 'more often than you would suppose'. A sample annual mailing plan might look something like this:

Example Annual Mailing Plan

A – appeal, R – annual report, I – information mailing/survey, U – upgrade mailing

	April	June	Aug	Oct	Dec
Committed givers	U	A	I	A	A
Major donors	U	R	I	A	A
Active donors	U	A	I	A	A
Lapsed donors	A	I	A		
Enquirers/prospects	A	I	A		

Botting Herbst and Norton 2012, p. 357

How long should we keep people on our mailing list if nothing appears?

As long as it is productive to do so. This is where it is enormously helpful to have good records and someone who is able to analyse them. What percentage response do you need to have to justify keeping names on the list? When it drops below that level, consider removing the names.

Where lists are of hundreds rather than thousands, you should be able to review each name individually, or at least those of them who have shown themselves to be most likely to give, or give larger amounts.

For example, Mrs Brown may have been a big donor in the past, so why not give her a ring and ask her if she is still interested? Mr Jones may have given one modest donation because he was asked personally by one of your former trustees at a council reception, but has shown no interest since – OK, off he goes.

Even in quite large charities, there can probably be a list of only hundreds of major donors who between them account for a large proportion of the income, and they can be treated individually even if all the others get automatically removed from the list after, say, four no-response mailings.

Isn't all this sounding a bit technical?

Yes, it is. Direct mail is one of the most technical forms of fundraising (because of this it is often all too attractive to those of us who are scared of making direct person-to-person requests, for which it is usually no substitute). There is a whole industry around the creation of direct mail packs, the measurement and testing of responses and the planning of mailing schedules, with commercial agencies whose sole business this is.

I think there are three main principles worth bearing in mind:
• Results depend on the quality of your list, not its size.
• Testing is of key importance; even the experts cannot tell in advance which letter will work and which will not.
• A genuinely moving personal letter can break all the rules! I remember one in which a lady was too embarrassed even to ask for money. She just wrote along the lines of 'It is all so terrible that I just feel I must tell everybody I can what is going on', and the money rolled in without her even asking for it. However, I don't recommend this approach as in most circumstances people must be asked.

Many modest-sized charities have a great advantage in that they can make their mailings much more personal than those from a professional fundraising department of, say, 30 staff.

How should we respond to enquirers?

Promptly, politely and personally will be enough to put you well ahead in the game, almost regardless of the actual content of your reply (though it should include a response form for those who would like to give a donation). Fundraising consultant Ken Burnett once sent out enquiries to the 20 largest charities from a fictitious would-be donor, Camilla Cole, asking for information. Less than half replied within a week, five of them took four weeks or longer to respond, 10% never answered at all and very few managed a personal reply (Burnett 1996). So you don't have to have any special magic; just be competent!

How should we respond to donations?

Promptly, personally and warmly. Another fundraising consultancy sent cheques for £15 each to 75 top charities and 19 of them sent no acknowledgement or thank you of any kind! Three hadn't even cashed the cheque within 12 weeks. Of those who did reply, some sent what was described as an 'impersonal and formulaic' letter of thanks that was 'little better than no thanks at all'.

How big do you really have to be before it becomes impractical for all your supporters to get a personally addressed and signed note from your chair or one of your trustees? And if your organisation is genuinely too big for this, why not from a senior staff member? After all, the donors are paying their salaries.

What about mailings to our existing supporters?

These are a bit different to cold mailings. Your aims are:
* to keep them giving, often by asking them to convert from occasional one-off donations to regular ongoing support. I would prefer to have a standing order for £25 a year than a single gift of £100;
* to encourage them to give more. This is often done by having special one-off appeals: 'Can you contribute to the rebuilding and expansion of our training centre?'

Can we ask for more money over and over again?

Well, yes, you can. It is easy to worry about sounding as if all you are after is the donors' money. Usually it is what you are after, and that is fine – though it is nice if you can also offer the option of becoming an active volunteer. The deal is that you have the ability to get something done that both of you think is valuable, and the donors have the ability to give money towards it. This makes you partners in the same rewarding enterprise.

Approach donors with an offer to enable them to join in something really worthwhile and satisfying and they will respond happily. The partnership is real. Without the donors, nothing would happen. So it is important to constantly recognise the partnership as such, in all your letters and literature. If a life has been saved, a family helped, a musician trained or a woodland preserved, they have done this just as much as you have. Donors are not external to your work; they are an integral part of it.

Therefore one purpose of your mailings is to keep your partners up to date with how you are doing, but you can also ask again for money at the same time. Just do it nicely – for example you can enclose a gift envelope with the suggestion that, if they are already doing all they can for you themselves, they might know of someone else who would like to join in the work.

Email appeals

The way in which you contact your supporters and potential donors by email should broadly follow the same principles as those for direct mail; however, there are a few obvious advantages to electronic communication.

Cost

Obviously, it's considerably cheaper to contact supporters via email, especially when you have a large contact list. Apart from the direct cost savings of not needing to pay for paper, postage and envelopes, it can save the indirect costs of people's time preparing, stuffing and mailing letters.

Easy to respond to

The recipient of an email can click a link to your online giving page and send you money via PayPal within a few seconds of receiving an email asking them to do that. If your message connects with them and you've convinced them to support you, it's incredibly easy on their part to do so. Contrast that with a letter that asks them (directly or indirectly) to find a pen, fill in the form, go and find their chequebook, write a cheque, put that . in the envelope, remember to take it with them next time they leave the house, and post it when they pass a post box. The opportunities for them to be distracted or delay their response are far greater.

Timeliness

An email appeal can be put together incredibly quickly. Topical or newsworthy issues can be quickly worked into the text of an email to support your case and make it easy for people to see the wider context of your work. You can also time emails in a way that is difficult to do with direct mail.

Testing

Probably the biggest advantage of email appeals is the fact that you can very easily test and measure the impact they have. Most basic mailing list tools will enable you to measure the open rate (how many people opened your email), the click rate (how many people clicked on a link in your email), bounces (how many of the emails on your list are not working or incorrect), and abuse reports (how many people marked your message as junk or spam). With that information you can continually test and retest your emails, even pre-sending emails to smaller test groups to see what the response rate is from different subject headings or content.

There are obviously downsides to email appeals though. It can be harder to be personal, they are easy to delete, and there is always a risk that too-frequent email appeals will end up pushing people away from supporting your cause.

Door-to-door and public collections

House-to-house collections are an effective way of raising money if you have access to a suitable pool of committed volunteers who are happy to undertake it. But this is a big 'if'.

Do we need permission to go house to house?

Yes, you need to get a permit from your local authority, and you need to have it at least a month before the collection is due to take place. If you are likely to be collecting in this way on a large scale and for an extended period of time, you can apply for a National Exemption Order. This is a one-off permit which will save you from having to apply for multiple permits in different local authorities; however, you need to have had collection licences in 70 to 100 local authority areas for the last two years to apply. The rules may change, but up-to-date information can be obtained from the Charity Commission (www.gov.uk).

Are there any rules about collecting?

Yes, lots, and they are all laid out in the House to House Collections Act (1939) and the House to House Collections Regulations (1947). The most important ones are:

- You must have a licence to carry out the collection, and it must be in place a month before you start collecting.
- The minimum age for a collector is 16.
- You must carry out due diligence to ensure that the collectors are 'fit and proper persons'.
- Every collector needs to wear an approved badge, a copy of the certificate of authority, and a sealed collecting box or receipt book.
- You must keep a record of the collectors' names, addresses, badges and certificates issued, and make sure they are all returned.

- If you're collecting for a charity with an income over £10,000 you must state that the charity is registered on any printed materials.
- A certified record of the funds raised must be kept, and submitted to the authority issuing the licence.

Your collectors need to be very well briefed and debriefed – the after-collecting gathering can also be a good little party in its own right. This is important because volunteers greatly value the social rewards they get from taking part in your collection. After all, there are very many other excellent causes they could do it for. They will tend to stick with the one that gives the most satisfying experience. It is not usually enough just to rely on commitment to your cause.

How do we organise the collection?

Conventionally, an envelope with an accompanying letter or brochure is dropped through the door. The collector then returns a few days later to collect the envelopes.

There are all sorts of options in terms of who does the collecting, what materials they might have as prompts or to leave behind with people they have spoken to, how much they might ask for, and any number of other variables. See the following case study about the Karuna Trust for examples of the kind of things to consider.

Case study: the Karuna Trust

Many years ago two people from the Karuna Trust came on one of our training courses; I was embarrassed as they knew far more about the realities of face-to-face fundraising than I did. The charity raises money in Britain for Buddhist welfare and educational projects in India. Done mainly house to house by young volunteers, I regard a successful spell with Karuna as one of the best qualifications a fundraiser can have.

Manjuka describes the operation as follows, though he does not mention that the fundraisers are backed up by some of the finest and most moving charity literature that I have ever seen, especially in its use of photographs (to be inspired, send an appropriate donation and get a copy of the latest annual report: details on www.karuna.org).

The Karuna Trust works in India amongst Dalit communities doing education, skills training, health and cultural projects. Karuna has been fundraising door to door soliciting Gift Aid Standing Orders for over 20 years [now over 30 years]. There are currently over 8,000 regular donors recruited in this way, providing a reliable income stream for the charity. These donors account for some 90% of an annual income of just over £1 million.

Karuna runs seven appeals annually, each lasting about six weeks with teams of up to seven fundraisers. Each appeal is in a different city, which is scouted ahead to find suitable areas – finding good areas is a bit of an art form, but the basic principle is that the exterior of a house says a lot about who lives inside. Obviously some people are more likely to sign up than others and therefore some houses are more likely to be worth knocking than others. The teams live together in a rented house and are guided through the experience by a leader from Karuna.

Our fundraisers are largely volunteers. As Karuna was set up and is run by Buddhists the volunteers are recruited from the Buddhist community so they tend to be self-aware, positive and communicative types, although they need not be extroverted – all temperaments can fundraise, what matters is their positive motivation. Ages have ranged from 20 to 74. Fundraising like this is an exhilarating experience. You never know what is going to happen next, who you are going to meet, how they will respond. It very much places you in the moment. If the fundraiser can embrace this experience with its attendant fears and uncertainties then they will be vibrant and interesting to the householders answering the door.

We just try and meet people and communicate with them. If a person is busy when we meet them on a door we notice and acknowledge that. The aim of the initial visit is to leave an introductory booklet that will allow the potential donor to consider whether Karuna is something they would like to support. The fundraiser then returns a few days later, once the potential donor has had a chance to think it through. Taking genuine interest and showing sensitivity and respect to householders is something most people appreciate and something which the trust in the long term benefits from. This creates a space into which they may become interested in Karuna.

To this end our fundraisers are trained in the art of communication. A range of training methods are used including role play, storytelling, games, body workshops, meditation. Approached in this way, householders are seldom rude or abusive to the fundraisers. Our approach results in many happy donors who invariably thank us for giving them the opportunity to give. We are so successful because we are like the bee that takes the pollen from the flower, leaving it unharmed with renewed potential to grow and develop.

Luke FitzHerbert and Manjuka 2003

What about street collections?

These are more difficult than house-to-house ones and seem to be declining. You will need a local authority permit, numerous volunteers for what is often seen as a rather unattractive chore and sealed collection devices. These last are available from commercial suppliers pre-printed with your logo and so on.

It is essential to have a proper system for collecting, counting and recording the money (for instance you must have at least two people there when the boxes are opened and the money counted and recorded).

It may be easier to have your collections in public places that are not streets, like shopping centres, where you just need the permission of the owners; but they may be reluctant to give this.

And face-to-face fundraising in the street?

This is highly successful and very controversial. It normally involves young people, employed by professional fundraising agencies, approaching members of the public in the street and asking them to commit to regular monthly donations by standing order or direct debit.

A few people complain vociferously about being harassed by relays of such people as they walk down the street, and the term 'chugger' (charity mugger) has unfortunately stuck.

It is highly expensive to get started, with most of the first year's donations usually going to the collecting agency, but as it brings in a high proportion of long-term supporters it can be well worth it.

It is, so far, confined to fairly large charities, especially those thought to be attractive to the relatively youthful donor – it was pioneered in Britain by Greenpeace – but this may be changing. The initial investment is nevertheless too high for many smaller charities.

For more information on the rules around street collections see the Institute of Fundraising's Code of Practice, section L6.2 Street Collections – England and Wales at www.institute-of-fundraising.org.uk.

Direct requests for donations

Just asking people for money, face-to-face or on the phone, is probably the most simple and straightforward form of fundraising. It is also quite threatening for many potential 'askers', who are embarrassed by the thought of talking to people about money – this is one reason why people are so tempted by any other form of fundraising that will avoid this situation.

It is essential to recognise that you are not asking for money for your own benefit, but for the children, or the ballet, or whatever. You also need to remember that the donor gets a lot in return – satisfaction of a kind that is much valued. So you are not a beggar seeking alms, but you are more like a salesperson offering something that people want – usually a warm and perhaps even unaccustomed glow of virtue – in return for the money.

In *Getting Started in Fundraising*, Michael Norton, the founder of DSC, quotes an example of the ideal approach, from Rtn G.M. Rao, former treasurer and volunteer fundraiser for the Bangalore Hospice in India: 'I am utterly shameless, I have no hesitation in asking my friends and persons to whom I am introduced for donations to a cause I believe in. After all, I am not asking for myself' (Norton and Culshaw 2000).

Won't we upset the people we ask?

This would be pretty unusual. You have complimented them by showing you believe them to be a generous person who might both like and be able to help a good cause.

How can we prepare for rejection or argument?

You could think about dealing with people's responses in the following ways:

- The person says 'sorry, no', with or without giving a reason. This will happen, no matter what you are asking for or how well you ask. It is quite OK for someone to say 'no' and they do not have to say why. You just thank them pleasantly for listening and move on (don't try to change their mind, at least, not on the spot). Remember, it is not you that is being rejected, but the proposition that you have put, and there are plenty more fish in the sea. Mostly the reason for the 'no' will be nothing to do with you or your charity anyway; it may be the letter from the bank that morning, the fact that the soup is about to boil over or because they are waiting for another call on the phone. Or they may genuinely be already wholly committed to supporting other charities.
- She or he asks questions you can't answer. Get fully briefed, if you are not already. Just go through with colleagues all the most likely questions. Then, if you get one that you did not expect, you can just say so, explaining what you do and do not know, and offer to find out and get back to them.

How can we get into this gently?

An excellent half-way house is to start with groups rather than individuals. For example, ask if you can come and talk to church groups, Women's Institutes and so on to explain what you are doing and ask for support. If you do this, it is always a great help to have pictures to show people, either by handing them round or using a projector (but the story still needs to be told).

The most successful appeal I ever saw was by a very young woman from a playgroup for disabled children in York. I had arranged for her to speak to about 80 engineering workers in a factory at their weekly staff training session. She said where she was from, 'the place down the road outside and on the left', and that unless they got some more money the playgroup would close and the children would have nowhere to go. She then burst into tears and ran out of the room, whereupon I collected 60 or so signatures for substantial donations.

Some people use videos so that they do not have to make the request themselves. That can be really effective, and can make it easy to make the appeal to a wide number of people, but it is also much less personal than asking for support face-to-face.

Does it become easy after a time?

For most of us, perhaps, it becomes much less difficult with experience (indeed after just the first one or two times), but no, it will probably never become easy. However, the kick when people agree to support your cause is terrific and more than enough reward even if it stays hard to do. It is so astonishingly productive and rewarding that this quickly comes to outweigh the nervousness we continue to feel. And you will enjoy the admiration and respect of all around!

There are indeed people who simply don't have any problem asking for money for a good cause, and they are worth their weight in gold. Getting them to support your charity, because you are such fun to work with, will probably be one of your aims.

Major gifts

This is where most fundraising began and is it is still a core fundraising component for many charities, especially those with access to a middle-class constituency.

For many of us, the problem is that society has become so physically segregated that there may be very few well-off people anywhere near where you are working. In such cases consider going to where the money is. If you are sitting in a room in Tower Hamlets listening to tales about everyone on the estate being unemployed or on a very low income, it may pay to focus your fundraising efforts to the tower buildings of the great banks in the City of London just up the road.

How do you bridge the gap between rich and poor, if this is what you want to do? There is no single way, but few groups are wholly without contacts to the better off. Churches are often a good meeting ground. In almost every area there are people with reputations for generosity and often with excellent contacts. Do not forget that such people are looking for you, in a general way, as well as you looking for them. They know that they have had all the breaks and are often seeking opportunities to share their good fortune with others who have not been so lucky.

What is a major gift?

For a small, wholly voluntary organisation it might be as little as £250. For a nationally known 'brand name' charity it might be as much as £10,000 or more.

They are often sought as part of a capital appeal (see chapter 5, page 63) but charities can also have a group of key regular supporters, perhaps called patrons or some other such title. In Oxford University they get recognition through, among other things, a public procession in spectacular academic gowns designed for the purpose.

In either case such gifts will usually come because the donor has been identified and personally asked for the gift by a trustee or a pretty senior member of staff – seldom by professional fundraising staff.

How do we seek such donors?

First, you work hard to make a list of possible major donors. They may come from among your existing supporters, they could be people already known for their generosity in your area or field of work, or they could just be identified by determined networking, usually by your trustees: 'I will ask Mrs Hudson; she knows every likely donor round here' and so on.

Second, you farm out the work of asking them, so that you have a list of who is to be asked by whom. This can be left to the askers to get on with in their own way (though they will need a lot of chasing, which should be your chair's job in many cases) or you can organise a social event that will give a good opportunity to ask at least some of them.

4 Events and fundraising activities

I have not headed this 'fundraising events' because many charity events meet more than one aim. Indeed the main aim may be to publicise your activities, with fundraising a secondary consideration. You have already seen an example in the Brent River Society case study on page 21.

Apart from that there are four main categories of event (though they can overlap):

- fundraising gatherings;
- 'pay-to-come' events;
- sponsored events;
- lotteries and games.

Can we raise money from social events?

While these events are an absolutely routine approach in American fundraising, for some reason they are less frequent in Britain – a pity as they are a straightforward way to raise money. You ask potential donors for a drink or a meal in your or another supporter's home – anything from a coffee morning to a barbecue – at which you explain what your charity is doing and ask for donations. People like to come as it will be a pleasant social occasion for a good cause.

Those invited need to be confident that they will not be pressed to give more than they can manage without pain. As invitations will generally be face-to-face or by phone, you can easily reassure people about this. One approach is to say that if they can't contribute significant money themselves, they are still welcome to come and help in some other way, by finding out about what they can do as volunteers, or by contributing suggestions of other people whom you might approach, or indeed just by helping run the event.

At the event, though, it is important to actually ask people to contribute – they are, of course, expecting this. However, it may be sensible to ensure in advance that the first person you ask will respond positively and generously.

There are many ways of organising such get-togethers. One spectacularly large-scale example is Macmillan Cancer Relief's 'World's Biggest Coffee Morning', which 154,000 people took part in in 2013, raising over £20 million (Macmillan n.d.).

Extract from The Hereford Times, 2015

Thursday, February 19, 2015   THE HEREFORD TIMES   9

Charity helped by bingo nights

BINGO nights at a Hereford pub raised hundreds of pounds for three charities.

The Air Ambulance received £1,000, while councillor Len Tawn was given £250 to put towards the Mayor of Hereford's good causes following the events at the Herdsman.

Cllr Tawn is supporting SSAFA (Lifelong support for our Forces and their families) and Retail Trust during his year in office. He is pictured thanking bingo organiser June Wright for her hard work.

Organiser June Wright with mayor Len Tawn

Reproduced courtesy of the *Hereford Times*.

'Pay-to-come' or 'pay-to-take-part' fundraising events

These again cover a huge range from the car boot sale on a school playground to the classical music recital with champagne supper in a country house.

Most local fundraising events, if they are to be cost-effective, need to be organised and managed by volunteers. Only larger, high-price ticket affairs justify hands-on management by professional fundraisers.

The big charities have what are called 'community fundraisers', a main part of whose job is to travel their area encouraging local volunteers to organise such events. Even so, neither the amounts raised nor the cost of raising them tend to be very attractive in themselves. The hope is more that they will attract new supporters who can be 'converted' into regular donors, especially those able to give bigger gifts or to write the charity into their wills. However, the substantial costs for big charities that don't have a local presence or connections can make the returns too low for this to be worthwhile.

On the other hand, charities with committed volunteers can often leave them to get on with it on their own, with only a limited investment of money or of the time of professional staff. Even here, though, it is easy for your trustees to put their scarce time into these often quite unrewarding activities, when they should be focusing on more productive ways of bringing in the money that is needed.

What about sponsored events?

I expect all of you have come across such events – 'Will you sponsor me for a three-hour silence?', or 'a marathon?', or a thousand other things. A more recent development is the sponsorship of individuals for what can appear to be little more than adventure holidays – climbing Mount Kilimanjaro or whatever. In some cases this has developed into something which is very close to trading, where the charity, usually through a trading subsidiary, becomes a holiday organiser and keeps the profits. However, these sorts of holidays are more often organised for the charity by a professional travel company.

What are 'subsidiary trading companies'?

All charities can trade as part of their charitable activities – DSC, publisher of this book and itself a charity, earns money from its publishing, training and events. As educating and informing people who work for charities is within its charitable purposes, this is no problem. But DSC could not earn money by selling its books to help commercial businesses manage themselves better; this would be trading outside its charitable purposes.

If DSC thought it could earn substantial money from such non-charitable publishing to support its charitable activities, it would have to set up a trading subsidiary to do so. This subsidiary company would then donate all its profits to DSC.

The field is complicated and professional advice is needed at an early stage. The situation is set out in full in the *Russell-Cooke Voluntary Sector Legal Handbook*, also published by DSC.

Case study: the Brent River Park barbecue

This was one of the first fundraising events with which I was involved. There is, in Hanwell, west London, a thatched cottage with a wood, a pond and a stream. The owner, herself on our committee, let us use this lovely and private place for a midsummer barbecue. Almost everything was provided free: tents and portable loos from the scouts, sound systems and DJs from local enthusiasts, tables and chairs from the church hall, square dance calling from the council water cleanliness officer who we knew otherwise in his professional capacity, and so on. Tickets were sold in advance, providing the cash with which to buy the food and drink.

The event ran successfully for years, with its own committee and little other input from the charity, and provided a good proportion of our annual income.

Luke FitzHerbert 2003

Managing an events programme

A key principle here is replicability. Successful events are usually a lot of work to set up the first time, but once established can usually be repeated annually (or more often) far more easily. Everyone knows what has to be done and they can just get on with it (though as people change and move, it is very much safer if a fairly detailed note of all the arrangements exists, even if only in the background).

The ideal is to have a portfolio of repeated fundraising events. For example, six events annually, with one new one being introduced and the least successful of the old ones being dropped.

Ideas for events are almost unlimited – just ask everyone to keep their eyes and ears open for what other people are doing and pick out the ones that attract you and your colleagues. An element of your own originality and imagination is very helpful, but it is unwise to risk much time or money on a totally new concept.

An attraction of events is that you can raise money for almost any cause in this way, either with events that are directly connected to your work or not. The London Great Gorilla Run, for instance, was an eight-kilometre run in London, put on by The Gorilla Organisation. Participants paid their entry fee, which included a gorilla costume to run in, and then raised money from friends and family. Or you could do something less connected to your work, like MENCAP's Four Pound Burger Challenge, which raises money by inviting participants to eat a gigantic burger.

Fund running

In recent years, there has been an explosion in the numbers of people raising money through running events, both directly and indirectly. The London Marathon is the largest fundraising event in the world, and has raised over £600 million since 1981 (Virgin n.d.). The marathon is hugely over-subscribed, but charities can become Gold or Silver Bond holders, which guarantee the charity places in the marathon that they can then give to prospective fundraisers who pledge to raise (usually well) over the amount the place has cost the charity.

The Race for Life series of races organised by Cancer Research has grown its women-only running events to include over 170 five-kilometre races across the UK, as well as races over other distances, including a marathon to be held in London in 2015. So far six million people have raised £493 million for Cancer Research through their races (Wikipedia 2014).

Raising money through running events isn't just the preserve of big charities. Many Rotary clubs for example organise their own races in order to raise funds for the local charities they support. There are hundreds of races of all distances taking place in the UK every month and many of them are put on in support of specific local charities, and many more are being run by individuals who are running for charities they have decided to support.

Some of those individuals can be very prolific fundraisers, such as 'Marathon Man' Rob Young who in 2014–15 ran 370 marathons in 365 days setting a new world record and raising over £50,000 for the NSPCC, Great Ormond Street Hospital and Dreams Come True. Tony 'The Fridge' Morrison has completed countless running challenges for charity, including running 40 marathons in 40 days to raise money for the Bobby Moore Foundation and from Land's End to John O'Groats, to raise funds for Newcastle upon Tyne's NHS Charity – all carrying a 40kg fridge.

Caution!

Some events carry big financial risks. One of my previous charity employers Weston Spirit was reliant on large gala-type events and sponsored adventure-type holidays, both of which carried large up-front costs that had to be met irrespective of the funds raised from them. Be very careful not to get into something that you cannot afford to see go wrong. It may pour with rain, or the celebrity entertainer may cry off, leaving you with all the fixed costs of the marquee, sound system and catering contract, or whatever. If it can happen, it will, sooner or later, and the possibility must have been allowed for.

Lotteries and games

All charity lotteries are regulated by the Gambling Commission, although it depends how big the lottery is as to whether you need a licence from them. Generally speaking, if you sell less than £20,000 worth of tickets per lottery, and less than £250,000 in any one year, you won't need a licence from the Gambling Commission (www.gamblingcommission.gov.uk), but you should check with your local authority, which may require you to have one.

Events and lotteries can be a successful and important part of a charity's fundraising, and occasionally the main or even the only part. However, often they are organised in place of the generally more effective straight pursuit of individual donations.

Although at first glance lotteries may appear to be an inexpensive option, they can be a costly way of raising money. A lottery still needs to attract people to play it, so you still have the costs of brochures, materials and postage, and that's before you factor in prizes and managing the whole process. If all of that work simply leads to people buying a £5 lottery ticket as opposed to making a £20 donation, which they might have made if you had asked them for that instead, a lottery can end up being less successful than hoped.

Note, however, that there is nothing wrong with activities such as events or lotteries having a high level of expenses, if these are incurred in providing prizes, parties or other benefits to the participants. The people who take part are paying for these benefits as well as making a donation to your charity. And if you do not offer good value, they will stop coming.

5 Capital appeals

What is a capital appeal?

This is usually a one-off campaign to raise money for a specific development, often a building, but it might also relate to a new programme or project. It is separate and additional to ongoing fundraising for the charity's day-to-day running costs.

Organising an appeal

Unlike most other forms of fundraising, there is a fairly well-established routine from which it would be risky to deviate too far. There are a number of stages:

- **Planning**. You will usually need a detailed plan for the work and its funding arrangements, often including a business plan or feasibility study. If you have limited experience of such a task, at the very least talk to people who have organised similar projects elsewhere.

- **Establishing an appeal committee**. These are committees of volunteers willing and able to ask for significant sums of money. Leadership is the key. The chair needs to be someone who will commit themselves to the appeal's success (not just a big name figurehead) and he or she will probably have previous experience of such appeals. You could try asking around to find who the active and successful members of earlier appeal committees in your area or field of work are – perhaps the time has come for them to lead their own.

- **Setting your targets**. It is usual to break down the donations required by number and size and then to write down the prospective donors for each band – assuming, perhaps, that you will need four prospects for each gift of a particular size, but allowing for another of the four to give a lesser gift. Suppose your new building will cost £1 million and you have been offered half of this amount from one of the Lottery funds, but must raise the other £500,000 yourselves. The table might look like this:

Amount	No. of gifts	Total
£100,000	1 donation	£100,000
£20,000 to £50,000	4 donations	£120,000
£10,000 to £20,000	10 donations	£130,000
£1,000 to £10,000	20 donations	£100,000
Less than £1,000	200 donations	£50,000
Total		£500,000

The plan may include some grants from trusts and foundations, or from other public sources, as well as from individuals.

- **Agreeing a programme of work.** Who will ask these people for their donations, where and how? There is probably a range of events to be organised, from private lunches to a public launch.
- **Implementation.** A substantial proportion of the large donations needs to be secured in principle before the campaign is publicly launched. This will give confidence to donors that they are associating themselves with something that is clearly going to succeed. If you cannot put the lead donations together in private discussions, you may have to rethink the whole appeal.

Using fundraising consultants

This is a field in which it may be worth talking to consultants, many of whom specialise in such appeals. They will normally come and talk to you free of charge in advance of any commitment and will probably be able to give you a useful and early view on whether or not your plans are realistic. You shouldn't be under any obligation to make any further use of their services.

6 Raising money from grant-making charities

Grant-making charities

Individual grant-making charities are often called 'trust' or 'foundation'. However, plenty are not, such as BBC Children in Need, and very many organisations with the word 'trust' or 'foundation' in their name do not make grants – the Terrence Higgins Trust, for example, is a fundraising charity like yours. You know them by what they do, not by what they are called.

How do we get grants from them?

You write and ask for a grant (or complete and submit their application forms), enclosing a copy of your annual report and accounts. They write back saying 'Yes' or 'No'. On average, about one in every three such letters results in a grant, although not necessarily for the full amount requested (DSC 2010).

For many charities this is the easiest, cheapest form of fundraising, but note two important cautions.

Two cautions!

1   Grants on their own will seldom produce enough income for any but the smallest, wholly voluntary, charities.
2   This is usually short-term money and cannot be relied on as regular support for the delivery of ongoing services or activities.

Researching a particular grant-making charity

Grant-making charities come in a huge range of shapes and sizes. Here are some of the ways one can differ from another.

Is it general or specialised?

*   The Tanner Trust (which has an annual grant total of about £396,000) gives around 135 grants a year, mostly of less than £1,000, to many kinds of charity: local, national and international.
*   The Cooks Charity (£220,000 a year) supports education in catering and in one year gives around 15 grants of £15,000 each.

Is it big or small?

The biggest grant-makers listed on DSC's www.trustfunding.org.uk website in 2015 were:

Wellcome Trust	£511 million	Biomedical research
British Heart Foundation	£124 million	Heart disease
The Sainsbury family trusts	£115 million	A range of very specific fields of interest
Oxfam	£91 million	Development and emergency relief
Leverhulme Trust	£80 million	Education and research
The Wolfson Foundation	£50 million	Medical and scientific research
Garfield Weston Foundation	£46 million	General, in the UK
Christian Aid	£46 million	Communities in the developing world
The Monument Trust	£45 million	Arts, heritage and health

DSC 2015

On the other hand there are thousands that give away less than £5,000 a year.

Does it make big grants or small grants?

The size of a grant-making charity doesn't necessarily tell you what size grants they give. The Parthenon Trust (expenditure £12 million in 2014) gives few grants of less than £50,000. The even larger Lloyds Bank Foundation for England and Wales (expenditure £21 million in 2014) give few that are for as much as that. Others, like Esmée Fairbairn Foundation, have a number of different programmes and in 2014 made grants ranging from £6,000 to £1.25 million.

Does it have an office and professional staff?

The mighty Sainsbury family trusts maintain a large and expert staff. The similarly sized Garfield Weston Foundation has very few. Most grant-makers have no staff at all and your letters are opened and dealt with by the trustees – all volunteers – and usually in their own homes.

When the grant total rises above £100,000 or so, many trustees begin to employ either a part-time administrator or they ask their solicitors or accountants to handle the correspondence and the making of payments, while the trustees still do the decision-making. Much bigger than this and you begin to see professional grant-making staff who investigate applications and advise trustees accordingly.

Does it have clear policies and guidelines?

Some grant-makers are clear and specific about what they will fund. Others say something like 'all applications will be considered on their merits', or say nothing at all – though they may well offer a list of what they will not fund. For example, funding from the Sherburn House Charity, in the Durham area, is to 'relieve need, hardship and distress' and it notes areas of interest such as health and disabilities or community needs, but it also has a list of 20 exclusions ('What we will not fund') such as 'organisations with substantial reserves or a serious deficit' or 'hospitals and medical centres (other than hospices)' (Sherburn House 2014).

Phrases such as 'guidelines for applicants' can mean almost anything. Many smaller grant-makers have none at all, or they are simply lists of what information is called for and how it is to be submitted, without indicating the policies of the grant-giving organisation at all. The following guidelines, from the MacRobert Trust in Scotland, is a good example of the typical type of grant guidelines you are likely to come across. It gives away in the region of £500,000 to £1,000,000 a year, mostly to Scottish charities. (NB The affection for capital letters is often found among grant-making trusts and foundations.)

Example guidelines: the MacRobert Trust

Themes & Sub-Themes

The themes and sub-themes define the scope of The Trust's charitable work under its Charitable Donations Policy. The themes are listed below. The sub-themes are detailed separately in the document at the bottom of the page and are not listed in any priority order.

Donations are given only to organisations registered as charities and are always dependent on funding availability.

Trustees reserve the right to make changes to the themes and sub-themes and to make judgements on applications which do not qualify for support.

- *Theme 1: Services and Sea*
- *Theme 2: Education and Training*
- *Theme 3: Children and Youth*
- *Theme 4: Science, Engineering and Technology*
- *Theme 5: Agriculture and Horticulture*
- *Theme 6: Tarland and the Local Area*

Guidelines

Applicants must adhere to the following guidelines when submitting their applications:

Timelines

- *Applications for the March Trustees' meeting must be submitted by 31st October of the previous year*
- *Applications for the November Trustees' meeting must be submitted by 31st May*
- *Late submissions will not be considered*

Time Bars

- *Unsuccessful applicants must wait for at least one year from the time of being notified before re-applying*
- *Successful applicants must wait for at least two years from the time of receiving a donation before re-applying*
- *When a multi-year donation has been awarded, the time bar applies from the date of the final instalment*
- *Withdrawn applications do not normally face a time bar*

Additional Guidance and Feedback

The following list of additional guidance and feedback is not exhaustive but can, from time to time, be useful for applicants:

- *Do not apply for a donation unless you are a registered charity in Scotland, England and Wales, or Northern Ireland*
- *Always include an informative covering letter and do not submit your application by email*
- *Some applicants fail to complete Part C2 of the application form, preferring to refer to attached documents. Please do not do this, as it places the burden on the reader and your application will probably not be considered any further. Instead, make sure a full explanation and justification of what is needed is included at Part C2*
- *As indicated on the application form, please do not provide more than one page of information for Part C2*
- *Provided you have argued the case in Part C2, feel free to include a small amount of additional, informative documentation*
- *Make sure the year or years for which the support is required is made clear in Part D1*
- *Given the lengthy lead times during the application process, applicants' financial circumstances can change significantly and donations may no longer be required. If this is the case, it is vital that you update The Trust as funds available for donation are always tight and money no longer needed can be directed elsewhere*
- *Do not seek to change your requirement late in the process. More often than not, this will not be allowed because applications are judged and prioritised against others, which may then need to take precedence*
- *If requirements change early in the process it may be worth asking if the thrust of the change can be made, particularly if the change is minor*

- *Above all, maintain a process of dialogue with us. We deal with many hundreds of worthy applications each year. If we have to chase you for information, you will understand that our interest might wane*
- *Make sure you sign your application as unsigned applications will not be considered*
- *Always check you have affixed the correct value of stamps to your application package. Incorrectly stamped envelopes may not be delivered to us and The Trust can incur additional postal charges. This will reflect badly on your organisation and your application may not progress further*

Exclusions

The Trust's revised Charitable Donations policy, introduced in November 2011, lists what we consider supporting.

Applicants should familiarise themselves with the charitable themes and sub-themes before making an application.

As a broad guide, applications are not normally provided for:

- *Organisations based outside the United Kingdom*
- *Beneficiaries resident outside the United Kingdom*
- *Individuals, except through The Trust's own training schemes*
- *General or mailshot appeals*
- *Political organisations*
- *Religious organisations*
- *Retrospective applications*
- *Student bodies as opposed to universities*
- *Departments within a university unless the appeal gains the support of, and is channelled through, the Principal*
- *Fee-paying schools, except through The Trust's own Educational Grants Scheme for children who are at, or need to attend, a Scottish independent secondary school*
- *Expeditions, except through the auspices of recognised bodies such as the British Exploring Society (Be)*
- *Community and village halls other than those in Tarland and the local area*
- *Pre-school groups, after-school clubs or school PTA's except where they lie in our local area*
- *Hospices, except where they lie in our local area*

Reproduced courtesy of the MacRobert Trust

Where does the grant-giving charity get its money?

Some grant-making trusts and foundations are 'endowed', that is they give away the income generated by their permanent and invested capital endowment which was the original donation by their founder – often through his or her will.

Sometimes the founder or founders may still be alive, in which case they may act more like a single wealthy donor rather than an institution of any kind. The Rausing foundations are much like this.

Other foundations earn or collect their money as they go along, like Comic Relief. These tend to be more formal in their grant-making, as they are answerable to those who put up the money.

How long does it take to get a decision?

Seldom less than two months, and often up to six months or even a year. Grant-makers are not a source of fast emergency funding (unless they already know you well and will treat you as an exception).

Grant-making

What do grant-makers like to fund?

It can be almost anything; just a straight donation to charities whose letters they like, a development or research activity, or a capital project like building works. Many appear to be policy-free, meaning that all applications will be considered on their merits, and they will not say what 'merit' consists of. Others are quite specific, either because of the way they were set up – the Trust for London (formerly the City Parochial Foundation) is for the benefit of the poor of London – or because of the sometimes very specific decisions of the current trustees – one of the many Sainsbury family trusts, for example, is concerned at present with the environmental effects of aviation, among other things.

What do grant-makers not like to fund?

Most often, and for good reason, grant-makers generally are reluctant to fund the ongoing costs of what you do. This is not their fault, but is inherent in the idea of grant-making in the first place. Their business is making funding decisions. In order to decide on new grants they must bring old ones to an end, otherwise they become silted up, just supporting the same charities every year and to that extent putting themselves out of the deciding business. But nevertheless a few have done exactly this, especially local grant-making organisations, and they support almost exactly the same charities year after year, while many others have at least a few old faithfuls whom they support indefinitely.

Unfortunately, few grant-makers like helping charities that have got into difficulties. Supporting the already successful is generally found more attractive!

Do we have to be skilled application writers?

I don't think so. You just need a good cause, presented in a way that you yourself would find convincing. Grant-makers rapidly become fairly good at extracting the gist of any application, and many quite dreadfully written applications result in grants. There is, however, a frequent distaste for the idea of professional fundraisers and if the application gives the impression of having come from such a source, this may count against it – grant-makers generally prefer to talk to the people who will be doing the work that they fund.

Grant-makers are regularly annoyed by applicants whose letters show that they have not even read the information available about what the funding body does.

Caution!

Read the guidelines! Research carried out by DSC has shown that around 30% of applications to grant-making charities are rejected because they fail to meet the basic eligibility criteria set by the grant-maker. This might be applications from charities in Wales to grant-makers that state they only fund in England, or applications for £30,000 when they state an upper grant limit of £10,000. Navigating your way past this simplest of tests before applying can increase your chances of success by a third, which has surely got to be the easiest way of improving your likelihood of success (DSC 2010).

Finding out about grant-makers

What information is available?

Many grant-makers produce some sort of guidelines for applicants, although even more do not. Where these exist, they must be read, but note that some grant-making charities take their own guidelines more seriously than others, and most make at least some exceptions to their own policies.

Only a minority of grant-makers has informative annual reports (though they all should do so, just like other charities) but nearly all now have a grants list with their annual accounts. These lists enable their policies to be deduced, at least to some extent.

For an example of an excellent set of guidelines, see www.tudortrust.org.uk. For a bigger website with more comprehensive information, including the full annual report and grants lists, try www.johnlyonscharity.org.uk.

How do we find it?

1   One of the best starting points is the grant guides published by DSC, the publishers of this book. Information on thousands of grant-makers is also available electronically from DSC's Trustfunding subscription website. (You can find information about these products on www.dsc.org.uk).

    In many cases these books will also direct you to the grant-maker's own website. The dedicated professional researcher may also use the Charity Commission register to look for any recent changes in addresses or trustees, or use the internet to research the background of individual trustees.

2   For many charities the full record of their dealings with grant-makers in the past, be they formal or informal, is particularly important as most grant-makers value a previous connection. Unfortunately, although grant-making charities usually have details accessibly filed about all your previous applications or grants, this is often not so the other way round. The lives of applicant charities are often turbulent, with record-keeping being a low priority. It is worth trying to reconstruct such a history if it is not readily available, especially where informal personal contacts were established. Knowledge of these past dealings may be more important than any paperwork.

3   Another excellent starting point may be to find out which grant-makers support other charities like yours by asking these charities.

From these sources it is usual to create a first list of your target organisations.

Which grant-makers should go on our 'target list'?

You need to find grant-makers that support your kind of work, or have a particular interest in your locality, or where you have or can develop a personal connection, and which have no exclusions that apply to you – 'no grants for physical disability', or whatever.

You can go to the books directly and just start reading through them, use their indexes, or use the search facilities on the trustfunding.org website. A word of caution, though, about these indexes: they can only be partially successful because many grant-makers supply such limited information that the indexing is inevitably a bit hit or miss. For serious fundraising, there will often be no alternative to a careful individual assessment of each possible grant-giver as far as your own charity is concerned. In no cases will the indexes give you a mailing list that you can use without actually reading about each individual organisation, especially its information on how to apply and on what is excluded.

If you do go straight to the books, one odd word of advice – do not start at A and work towards Z. We once found that of two very similar grant-making charities, the one at the start of the alphabet was getting twice the number of applications as the one at the end. Presumably many people started at the beginning and never got to Z, I hope because they were already getting all the grants they could handle.

Applying for grants

Should we talk to them first?

Yes, do this whenever it is sensible, but only after reading all their published guidelines (if these exist). To do otherwise can greatly annoy people (although your first call may simply be to ask for an up-to-date set of guidelines, or even to enquire if they have any).

Won't they just say 'send in your application'?

Some will, which is fine, but more and more grant-makers actively encourage such calls – after all, they may be able to dissuade you from sending in a hopeless application which would waste their time as well as yours. But with others, they may have a published dislike of preliminary phone calls, there may be no published phone number, or the number may be that of a purely administrative intermediary, like a firm of accountants which actually plays no part in deciding on the grants. And beware, you may think you are ringing an office, but it may well be a voluntary trustee on her or his home number for whom the trust's affairs are just a very small part of a busy life.

What kind of calls do they like?

By and large they welcome sensible calls and much dislike time-wasting ones – of which they say they get quite a few.

What is a sensible call?

It will vary according to the information available, but it could be something like one of the following (depending on the published information available).

'I have read your guidelines and we have two kinds of work that we can ask you to support. Can you tell me which of them your trust is more likely to find interesting?'

'I can send you a full 36-page proposal complete with business plan, or would you just prefer a simple letter at this stage?'

'When do I need to get you my application for it to go to the next trustees' meeting?'

What is the kind of call that annoys them?

Asking a question to which the answer is already published in their guidelines, on their website or in the trust directories.

How many applications should we send in?

It's up to you, but the more you ask, the more you are likely to get. If your chances of success are one in four, then to approach only three grant-making charities means you are most likely to receive nothing.

Do they have application forms?

Sometimes. Generally speaking the larger the grant-maker the more likely they are to have a more formal application process with a form and specific guidance, although some large grant-makers will be more informal and some small ones more structured.

Sometimes there is a form to make sure you give the basic information, which has to be backed up by an explanation of what you are asking them to support. If they have a form, make sure you use it. Your application won't be the only one they receive, and if the trustees or grant administrator has 50 nice neat forms to read though, with the information they need all in the same place on every one, except yours, you are going to stand out, and not in a good way.

Caution!

Many trustees do not want 'funding applications', just letters to themselves. They value the personal and tend to dislike the institutional. Wouldn't you, if, say, it was a family trust in memory of your grandad? I hear many complaints about inappropriate language: 'Who do they think we are – a local authority?'

What should we say in our letter?

If the grant-maker spells out what it wants you to send, send it. Otherwise it depends on who you are writing to. This can vary from a trustee of a family trust who opens your letter at the breakfast table to a harassed administrator handling many applications for small grants and with little time to spend on each, to experts in your field who are looking for the best investments for their money.

If what you want to do is simple and self-explanatory, does your community centre need to say any more than the following?

> Can your trust give us £10,000 so that we can continue our lunch clubs for more than 30 isolated elderly people every day? The problem is that our ancient kitchen has been condemned – rightly – and it will cost this much to put it right. I attach details of the repairs that are needed, who we are and what we do.

How long can our letter be?

We have already covered some of the general points on letter writing on pages 41–44. Trusts are not much different, except that they are already committed to giving money away to some charity, even if not yours, and so get many letters. Though they are seldom swamped by them as they often complain – it would be unusual even for a large grant-maker to receive more than eight applications in a working day – they do feel swamped and take every opportunity to ask applicants to make their letters shorter.

My experience is that shorter applications are also better in other respects, provided all the requested information is also attached.

I have never come across an application so complicated that the request cannot be expressed on a single, uncrowded page, although I am told that unfortunately few succeed in being as short as this. You can attach as much detail as you like, or as is called for, but in my experience decisions are far more often based on immediate reactions rather than on detailed study (although this immediate reaction may then be modified if the backup material, such as your accounts, is absent or too weak).

I suggest that the single page might include the following.

- At the start, if possible, explain **why you are writing to them** (as opposed to sending a 'circular' letter to every grant-maker you can think of): 'I am writing because five years ago you gave us a badly needed grant for …'; or '… at the suggestion of your grateful grant-holders at xyz charity'; or '… because your trust is an important supporter of work for the rights of …'; or '… at the suggestion of Mrs …, whom I believe you know' or '… following our brief conversation on the phone yesterday'. Even a minimal thing like this means your letter is unlikely to be seen as a circular.
- Also at the beginning, in just one sentence, say **what you want**: 'Will you give us £x for y?' (Otherwise they will just start skipping to the end to see what you are asking for.)
- Say **what the problem is** that a grant from them will address – this should normally be your beneficiaries' problem, rather than your organisation's problem. For example, 'with £10,000 we can ensure the future of lunch clubs for hundreds of isolated elderly people every year' rather than 'with £10,000 we can rebuild our community centre's kitchen which has been condemned by the health and safety inspector'.
- Describe **what you will do** about the problem: 'With the £10,000 we will not only meet all the new regulations but we will do it in a way that enables the old people themselves to play a far larger part in preparing the meals – which they greatly enjoy.'
- Explain **how you arrived at the figure you are requesting**: 'I attach a copy of the costings; we have been able to get the price down to £9,000 from the original estimate of £16,000. I hope that you will agree that another £1,000 for contingency costs is also prudent.'
- **Repeat the request**: 'We do hope you can give us this grant. If you can, the elderly club members will be so relieved – for many, it is the main part of their entire social life.'
- Note the attachments you are enclosing.

What about tone, style and appearance?

- This is a personal letter, not a business letter. Neither you nor they are businesses and a business style is inappropriate and off-putting, especially for trustees who widely deplore what they see as an increase in fundraising professionalism at the expense of what they see as personal commitment. In my view, for most charities, the letters usually come best from your own trustees (provided the trustee is closely concerned with the work in question). If no trustee is sufficiently involved, then it should come from the most senior person closely concerned with the issue.

- You should avoid the appearance of the word-processed, mail-merged appeal – you know the sort of thing, perhaps: 'You will remember, Mrs J. D. Martin, ...'. Always try to find a named person to write to, rather than 'Dear Sir or Madam'.
- Another useful way to make the letter more personal is to write by hand what can safely be written by hand – the date, the salutation, the sign off (Yours sincerely, or whatever) and, of course, your name.
- Style. You have choices to make! See the examples in the following box.

Example: the style of application letters

Here are two ways of saying the same thing in a letter to a family trust (the first being the one that was actually used):

In the past your trust has donated generously to our organisation, for which we were most grateful. ... We have now been in existence for six years and during that time we have supported 198 families. Our main funding now comes from the Blankshire County Council Social Services Department and this has gradually increased over the years to approx. 75%. ... We now have a shortfall of £5,000 up to April next and would ask to be considered by your trust for financial help towards this shortfall ... We have recently entered into a service agreement with Social Services which we hope will eventually lead to 90% funding from them.

This is very formal. The following would generally be better:

You helped us before in 20xx with a grant of £xxx. We are now planning to help even more families, but need your help again to do so.

Happily, we are working towards regular 90% funding from the Council for this work and have already got the figure up to 75%.

However, to get to the next stage we need to put in another £10,000 of our own this year. Can you help us with this?

Personally, I would probably put this kind of information on a separate attachment anyway – 'The Financial Situation' or such like – rather than in my letter. Try to be simple and straightforward. Avoid jargon and long words, sentences or paragraphs. Put the detail in appendices.

Above all, if you feel strongly about the importance of what you are asking for, let this show. Grant-makers wish to support those who feel strongly about the worth of what they are doing, but the tone of many of the letters they get is cool to the point of glaciation.

- Appearance. You say you are wonderful, but then you would, wouldn't you? About the only thing the grant-maker has to go on is the appearance of your letter and enclosures. It is worth a lot of effort to get a letterhead, annual reports, leaflets and so on that are unexpectedly impressive for your kind of organisation – and don't look too expensive. Quite a challenge and one that will usually only be met by a first-class graphic designer being pushed to produce his or her very best work.

What attachments should we include?

Note first that any attachments usually serve as back-up information; the top letter or the summary on the application form is generally what counts most. I am regularly asked to look at 'applications' in which the actual application is missing and where I am only sent the back-up stuff.

Many grant-makers are quite specific about what they want. Follow their guidance carefully. Otherwise, grant-makers normally expect to see a copy of your most recent annual report and accounts (unless your organisation is too new to have these yet). You may also want to add, if it seems appropriate to you, or refer to the existence of:

- evidence about the need for or effectiveness of your work;
- an independent note of endorsement from someone with no axe to grind: 'I know these people and their work, and it is wonderful' from, say, the bishop or the chair of the local bench of magistrates, or a noted celebrity with a relevant connection to your cause;
- a business plan, especially if there are building works involved.

Caution!

I believe that most trust or foundation money (usually accounted for by a relatively small number of the bigger large awards) is given in grants to people who the organisation already knows, likes and has confidence in, and where the written application serves largely to confirm an understanding previously arrived at in a more informal way.

Establishing such ongoing working relationships needs to be a key long-term objective for charities that expect to need the same sort of support in the future as well as right now. However, until such a relationship is established, your application, plus perhaps one advance telephone call, is usually all there is.

Case study: getting grants from grant-making charities

Simon Pellew set up and ran Pecan, a highly successful charity training unemployed people in South London which now itself employs nearly 100 people. He subsequently became the Chief Executive of Stepping Stones, providing accommodation and care for ex-prisoners, and is now the Chief Executive of the Society of Analytical Psychology. He took part in one of DSC's early fundraising training courses and back in 2002 he offered the following advice from his own experience:

When I started Pecan, 14 years ago, I read through the trust directories and felt that with so much money around I would easily ... find people who would give me the money I needed to make my fantastic idea work.

So, I produced a beautiful leaflet (at a cost of about £2,500) and a detailed description of my idea and sent it out. I got nothing back. This dented my confidence somewhat and made me suspect that there weren't hundreds of people out there just longing to give me money. I realised I would have to work at it.

What advice would have saved me from making these painful mistakes? First, get some training. The DSC Effective Fundraising course's ... listing of our possible 'selling points' [see page 22] opened my eyes to how to 'sell' the charity; and ... actually realising they weren't interested in my organisation, but in what we were going to do, transformed my approach.

Secondly, don't say to yourself 'I only need one donor to give me £x thousand ...'. It doesn't work like that. No one is likely to give you more than 50% of your costs, and probably only a third. Also, don't ask for too much; if you are a new charity no trust is likely to give you more than half their average donation (this is my rule-of-thumb but it seems about right).

Thirdly, keep the asking letter short and simple. I wrote too much and I spent too much money on producing a flash leaflet. Much better to keep it very simple. Remember that these trusts get lots of applications every day. When you write your application, picture the poor person doing the initial sift through that day's pile and think how to make your letter easy for them to read and understand.

Fourth, start with a number of small, general trusts. There will probably be one or two really large trusts whose donations' criteria you fit perfectly. You really want to succeed with these and so it is better getting a bit of practice on less important trusts first. Once you start getting some money back you know you have got a reasonably good asking letter, and then you can write for the bigger sums.

One of the great joys of fundraising is opening a letter and finding a cheque. But, to experience it, you always have to remember that people need to be persuaded to be parted from their hard-earned money.

Simon Pellew 2002

What should we do if they give us a grant?

Assume that this will be the start of a long-term relationship (or will help to continue an existing one).

- Immediately acknowledge receipt of the grant, always in writing but, where appropriate, personally as well.
- Immediately cash the cheque (if that is how the payment is made).

It is sad how very many charities are unable to manage these elementary courtesies.

Why your funders become your partners

This does not just apply to grant-makers, but it is often most obvious with them. Once they have given you a grant, donors have bought into your work. Your success becomes their success and any failure by you would show their judgement to have been poor – if you fail, they have been stupid. So they have a built-in interest in helping you. From the moment you get a grant or a substantial donation, you will usually be able to talk to them on a quite different basis – that of partner to partner, rather than of supplicant to funder.

Indeed most grant-makers talk happily about the advantages to both sides of having a relationship and say that this is the long-term key to successful fundraising from grant-giving organisations. Talk to them about your hopes, fears, disappointments and ideas for the future.

One thing that is important to remember, is that grant-giving trusts and foundations are charities too. Their objectives are (hopefully) similar to yours, whether they are the relief of poverty, supporting young people, or promoting the performing arts. The only difference is that the way they achieve those objectives is to give money to organisations like yours. Grant-makers can get frustrated when they are treated like a cash-machine, or a bank, and rightly so. For them, as it is for the organisations they fund, the money is simply a means to an end, not the reason they exist. Without applicants to carry out the work, they are useless, as are many of us without their support, and showing an appreciation of that during your early exchanges with them can go a long way to building a strong and productive relationship.

Small grants

A grant of less than £5,000 is usually regarded in the world of the big grant-makers – though not of smaller ones – as a 'small grant', although most of their small grants are for a good deal less than this.

In general, there is some reluctance to give even these grants for regular ongoing costs such as salaries or rent. In such cases it may be best just to ask for a donation towards the cost of the work being done. (See page 27 for information on how to go about doing this.)

There are many grant-makers that make large numbers of small grants, details of which can be found in the grant guides or online databases produced by DSC and others.

If your organisation is new to fundraising from grant-giving trusts and foundations, why not start off by seeking some small grants before you try for the big time? You might get some money to help with your set-up costs, to get decently designed letterheads and literature, or for some initial training to prepare yourselves for what you are getting into.

Some grant-makers have a simple application form, such as the Big Lottery Fund which is outlined below. For others, all that is needed is a simple one-page letter with a copy of your annual report and accounts.

The National Lottery

Lottery money is distributed by numerous separate organisations – arts councils, sports councils and the Heritage Lottery Fund – most of which can be accessed by at least some charities through a wide and varied range of funding programmes. These are part of public expenditure, subject to Treasury regulation and so on, and are outside the scope of this book – and generally we call it funding rather than fundraising (you can get full information on all of them via www.lotterygoodcauses.org.uk/funding).

However, the Big Lottery Fund (also known as BIG) administers a range of programmes that are specifically aimed at meeting the needs of charities and which act like grant-making trusts and foundations. They therefore deserve exploring here.

The Big Lottery Fund

BIG is responsible for distributing 40% of all funds raised for good causes by the National Lottery, around £670 million in 2014. Since it launched in 2004 it has given over £8 billion to projects supporting health, education, environment and charitable purposes, from early years intervention to commemorative funding for World War Two veterans. Their funding supports people who want to make life better for their communities, delivering funding throughout the UK, mostly through programmes tailored specifically to the needs of communities in England, Scotland, Wales or Northern Ireland, as well as some programmes that cover the whole of the UK (BIG n.d.). They also act as a grant administrator for Civil Society, managing the application and grant making processes for some of their funding programmes.

Its vision, outlined in its Strategic Framework 2015–21, is 'People in the lead', and their funding programmes during this period will be focused on helping people to build and renew their communities. New programmes will emerge throughout this time, but a proportion of BIG's funding will always be demand-led and lightly prescribed and should therefore be available to all charities with suitable projects which meet the outcomes of the various relevant BIG programmes. One of the main BIG programmes is called Reaching Communities England, which has £150 million available for any project which fits the following outcomes;

- People having better chances in life, with better access to training and development to improve their life skills.
- Stronger communities, with more active citizens working together to tackle their problems.
- Improved rural and urban environments, which communities are better able to access and enjoy.
- Healthier and more active people and communities.

Reaching Communities England gives grants from £10,000 upwards. There is no upper limit but you need to contact them before applying if you plan to apply for more than £500,000. Unlike previous Lottery grants for charities they can consider funding existing work providing longer-term sustainable funding is planned from another source.

How do we apply?

In order to apply for this fund you must first complete an outline proposal form which you can download from www.biglotteryfund.org.uk. If you are successful you will then be sent a full application. If your outline proposal is rejected the first time you are able to reapply.

The assessment is based on the 'outcome funding' approach. It is therefore essential that you write from the perspective of what your project will achieve, rather than what it will do. There is considerable guidance available on the BIG website, including advice on aims and outcomes: showing how your project will make a difference, but they also run a Big Advice Line, so you can contact them by phone if there is anything you are unsure of.

Two cautions!

1   If your work helps everyone, including the prosperous, such as, say, a bereavement counselling service, it may be difficult to get a grant towards your work as a whole. You will probably need to have a project specifically aimed at bringing your counselling to those at greatest disadvantage.

2   Experience of dealing with other Lottery distributors, such as the arts councils, is of limited relevance when seeking grants from the Reaching Communities Fund. They have completely separate systems and cultures. Also beware of consultants offering to prepare your application for you. If the information and detailed project planning is to hand, the application is not too hard to fill in yourselves. If it is not, expert application writing is unlikely to cover over the gaps.

Awards for All small grants

Awards for All is a small grants programme that gives groups an easy way to get small Lottery grants of between £300 and £10,000. The programme funds a wide range of community projects aimed at developing skills, improving health, revitalising the local environment and enabling people to become more active citizens. It is open to a much wider range of groups than other Lottery programmes, so community groups, parish councils, and schools can apply, as well as registered charities.

The only formal requirement is that you have a bank account into which the grant can be paid. The types of activities that they will fund include:

- putting on an event, activity or performance;
- buying new equipment or materials;
- running training courses;
- setting up a pilot project or starting up a new group;
- carrying out special repairs or conservation work;
- paying expenses for volunteers, costs for sessional workers or professional fees;
- transport costs.

Application forms can be downloaded from the BIG website, and submitted via email. They will let you know whether you've been successful within about ten weeks, but you should apply at least four to five months before you want your project to start.

7 Raising money from companies

Getting companies to give

This is usually more difficult than getting grants from trusts and foundations, so it may be best to leave it until your trust fundraising programme is fully developed, unless you have particular opportunities in this field.

Caution!

Corporate fundraising gets far more attention than is justified by the amount of money available. No doubt this is because, when a company is generous, it has a PR department whose job is to shout the good news from the housetops. No other source of funding has this ballyhoo behind it. If your charity is getting very little from companies, don't necessarily worry. It is likely to be the same for most other charities in similar positions to yours.

How do companies give money to charities?

In three ways:
- in donations;
- by their staff raising money for your charity;
- through corporate sponsorship.

Can we get donations or grants from companies?

You can ask. According to *The UK Civil Society Almanac*, corporate donations and gifts in kind totalled about £933 million in the UK in 2011/12, compared with two and a half times as much from grant-making charities. They come from the profits of the company which would otherwise go to its owners, the shareholders. Unlike grant-making charities whose objectives are purely charitable, companies' first responsibility is to make a profit for their shareholders. Whether or how they give after that varies enormously. Companies may set up formal giving programmes to redistribute a proportion of their profits, or their shareholders may give nothing at all via the company, preferring to take the maximum dividends and then give to causes (or not) as individuals. Many will fall somewhere in-between giving formally and giving nothing, and finding out the best way to get a specific company to support your cause can require quite a bit of research.

Nevertheless, if there is a particular reason why a company might support you, it is always worth asking. For example:

- You may have friends among the company's staff who will support your application.
- There may be a connection between your work and the company's activities. For example a utility company trying to avoid bad publicity when they have to disconnect non-payers might support your money advice service, or Samaritans' work with Network Rail to prevent suicide on the railways.
- There may be a local connection. For example, perhaps they are a major local employer and you support their pensioners in their old age.
- The company may have a donations policy that fits what you do. For example, 'We support technical education'. So do you.

How do we ask for a donation?

If possible, personally, backed up by a simple letter, like those to grant-making charities but much, much shorter – one or two paragraphs (you can enclose back-up materials). Unlike a grant-making organisation, supporting charities is not a company's proper business. They get their living by making widgets or whatever and your letter is a distraction from this.

Who do we write to?

For very big companies with a formal giving programme, there is often an open application process much the same as you would find with a large grant-making charity. Detailed information on the largest 400 companies that give in the UK are set out in *The Guide to UK Company Giving* (for more information see www.dsc.org.uk/gcg). For local or smaller companies, or for local branches of bigger ones, I recommend a telephone call to find out who best to approach. In the absence of any other suggestions, I would usually ask for the managing director's personal assistant or equivalent.

How can we get a company to fundraise for us?

By asking. Many companies 'adopt' charities and their staff raise money for them. The company may chip in some of its own money as well. Sometimes this is just for a year or whatever, sometimes it is ongoing: 'We have always supported them'.

Corporate sponsorship

What is sponsorship?

Sponsorship is quite different, at least in principle. You do a deal with a company in which they get something valuable from you, usually publicity or PR benefits of some kind, in return for their money. The money will usually come from some kind of marketing or PR budget, rather than being a gift out of its profits.

So consider what you may have to offer a company. If they sponsor your annual report, with their name on its cover, will that be valuable positive publicity for them? At a local level, this could be the case for any business that advertises in the local paper, say. You offer them a comparable amount of publicity for a similar price.

Nationally, an association with a major charity can indeed make a company look and smell sweeter than would otherwise be the case. The biggest companies have sponsorship managers, departments and budgets. But be careful. These people are 'buyers', out to get the most good publicity for their company in return for their money and it is becoming a pretty competitive market. All too often, not much is left for the charity after it has generated all the agreed benefits for the sponsor.

Caution!

Sponsorship can sometimes be most easily had from those by whom you would least wish to be sponsored – tobacco or food companies sponsoring health charities, big polluters sponsoring environmental activities and so on. Even leaving the moral issues to you, is it worth the risk to your reputation?

How do we get sponsorship?

By suggesting that you submit a 'sponsorship proposal' setting out what you will do and what the benefits will be for the company, in return for the payment you name. Then you negotiate. See the following box for an example.

Example: a theatre's sponsorship offerings

A theatre offered:

- sponsorship of a show for the duration of its run, credited to your company
- up to 20 complimentary dress circle tickets, with a discount of £2 on any additional tickets purchased;
- a display in the theatre's foyer;
- opportunities to invite cast members to attend post-event receptions;
- arrangements for complimentary use of the restaurant or the Langtry Room;
- name and logo on the theatre's website (www.everymantheatre.org.uk);
- tour of the theatre after the show;
- publicity and PR opportunities;
- print accreditation (name and logo) on:
  - 70,000 full-colour season brochures;
  - 1,000 season playbills;
  - two giant billboards outside the theatre;
  - production-specific posters and leaflets;
  - production programmes, with full-page complimentary advertisement;
  - press/media advertisements for the show;
  - press releases for the show.

For further information on corporate sponsorship see chapter 11 in *Corporate Fundraising* and for contact details of the relevant people in larger companies, see the listings in *The Guide to UK Company Giving*, (both published by DSC, www.dsc.org.uk). Locally you will just have to network.

Non-financial help

Increasingly companies are looking for ways to support charities that are more in line with their areas of business. The most high-profile example of this in recent years has been the partnership between Samaritans and Network Rail, aiming to reduce suicides on the railways. Both organisations had a clear interest in a shared outcome, and by working together, with Samaritans providing training in Managing Suicidal Contacts and Trauma Support, they are able to have a much bigger impact on the issue than if Network Rail simply gave them money. These kind of high-level partnerships are out of reach for most smaller charities, but the principle can be applied more locally. For example, to improve road safety in your local area you could apply for a grant or donations from local businesses, and spend that money on signage, or running road awareness programmes with local schools, with the outcome of reducing the number of traffic accidents. Or you could meet with local businesses, especially those making or receiving deliveries, and convince them of the benefits of them re-routing or changing the times of their deliveries so as to avoid local hotspots like schools at specific times. You may achieve the same outcome without needing any money, and actually, by changing the underlying behaviour, the effects of your intervention may last even longer.

Caution!

The high street companies get more requests than anyone else. You may get on better with other employers less in the public eye, such as the big wholesaler on an industrial estate, or the clerical offices of a credit card company.

8 Raising money online

The internet and digital technologies present a whole range of opportunities for fundraisers. Social media can be used to identify and reach potential donors quickly and cheaply, as well as provide a means to engage them more effectively with your work. A timely and well-articulated message can quickly spread and, combined with the ease of online donation sites, bring in huge amounts of income for your cause, as the Amyotrophic Lateral Sclerosis (ALS) ice bucket challenge has shown.

With free and simple-to-use website building tools like Weebly and Wordpress it is easy and free for even the smallest organisation to have an online presence. The benefits this brings can be significant in having a place to direct donors to specifically, and for people to find you for themselves. It also opens up a whole world of other fundraising possibilities.

There are a range of online tools and platforms that can assist you, not all of which will be relevant or desirable, and not all of which will still be in existence in a few years' time. However, the following areas, if not the specific examples, are likely to be around for a while, and are certainly worth examining in the context of what you are trying to achieve for your charity.

How can social media help us?

Social media can be a really useful tool for you in a number of ways. It brings the cost of communicating with existing and potential donors down to almost nothing, and can give your organisation a (theoretically) unlimited audience. Engaging your existing donors via a Facebook page or Twitter account and encouraging them to share your stories and requests for support with their friends, can quickly draw in many new supporters. LinkedIn is aimed more towards professionals and organisations, but again can provide useful contacts and start new relationships.

As a fundraiser the thing to remember with social media is what do you actually want to achieve? Go back to those core questions about who you are trying to reach, and with what message, and then plan accordingly. If you are looking to attract major corporate donors, for example, a Facebook page is unlikely to do that. You might, however, find that the

CEO is on Twitter or LinkedIn, and are able to make contact with them directly much more easily than the more traditional route of asking for a meeting.

If your target is to increase legacies from donors over the age of 60, Twitter is probably the wrong place to either find or engage with them, but there are over 194,000 people in the over-60s community group on Facebook.

What about online giving platforms?

There are a whole range of websites you can sign up to so that people can make donations online to your organisation. Generally speaking, they all work the same way. Your charity registers its details and gets a page on that giving site. Then your charity can link to that page, or get the code or widget to put a donation function straight onto your own website. It also means donors can set up their own giving pages for sponsored events and share with their friends, but the funds are directed to your account.

The benefits of doing this can be huge, connecting the reach you can have online to a quick and easy way for people to donate, and once set up it takes little work to maintain or administer, especially as they can take care of the Gift Aid element of donations received too. However, of the organisations providing these services, there are some differences to be aware of.

Givey (www.givey.com) passes on 100% of the donation (including Gift Aid) and charges no sign-up or transaction fees, but most other sites charge either a one-off registration fee (Virgin Money Giving), a monthly fee (Just Giving), or take a cut of either the donation or the Gift Aid element of it (MyDonate, Charity Choice, Every Click).

How can we take advantage of mobile phone giving?

Many online giving platforms (for example Just Giving's JustTextGiving) also offer text donation services, which enable charities and individuals to receive donations via SMS (Short Messaging Service). They are set up in much the same way as other online giving accounts, but instead of (or as well as) being issued with a web address to direct donors to, you will receive a simple code that links to your account, and a short number for the donor to send it to. When the person wanting to give responds to your request, for example, 'To donate £3, text BEAT to 70200', you will receive the donation, and the donor will pay through their mobile phone bill.

This can be a really good way for you to ask people for support because the call to action is about as straightforward as it is possible to get. It can be especially useful in public campaigns (using, say, posters, billboards or bus stop advertisements) where a request to text a simple number means they can respond there and then, rather than you relying on them to remember your campaign poster when they get home and to look up your website. It also doesn't rely on people having their credit or debit card details to hand, or require them to be online to give, and with 93% of adults in the UK owning or using a mobile phone there are no real technological barriers to donors giving in this way (Ofcom 2014).

How does crowdfunding work?

The idea behind crowdfunding is simple, you set out what you want to achieve, provide, build, or create, and ask people to pledge an amount of money up-front so that you can do it. When enough people have pledged and you've reached your target, off you go. While sites like Kickstarter (www.kickstarter.com) are predominantly filled with entrepreneurs looking for seed funding, there are specific socially focused crowdfunding sites, like www.crowdfunder.co.uk where you can post your specific campaign or target and ask for contributions.

This method of raising funds works best with specific tangible requests, and sometimes involves offering those backing the project some kind of incentive linked to the level of their donation. A whole range of organisations and projects have been successful, from The Nightshelter in Cardiff raising over £21,000 to cover the cost of running their homeless shelter for 12 months, to the Camberley Community Group Garden Project that raised £380 to rebuild their garden for disabled adults after it was destroyed by vandals.

You'll need to think carefully about the target you set as you will only receive the money pledged if you reach it, and there are fees to pay out of the money raised should you be successful, but it can still be a very productive and engaging way to raise funds. The process of explaining what you want to achieve, telling people what you need from them, and asking them to be a part of it – all good fundraising practice – is central to this way of raising money, and if you can do it well it can put your work in front of people who are actively looking for causes or projects to support, but who would otherwise not know anything about you.

What about social lending?

Social lending follows a similar model to crowdfunding. Organisations such as Kiva (www.kiva.org) and Zidisha (www.zidisha.org) are among the most established social lending websites.

How it works is that social entrepreneurs, most usually in developing countries, post summaries on the social lending website of what support they need, provide a brief business case or explanation of how the loan will be repaid, and then individual investors (who can be anyone like you and me) make a decision to loan some or all of the money they are asking for. The loans tend to be limited to relatively small amounts, aimed at giving individual social entrepreneurs the skills or tools they need in order to generate income for themselves, and to pay back the loan finance. Requests for loans to buy things like agricultural supplies, fertiliser, pesticides, sewing machines, water purification systems and construction materials are common.

While this type of funding is not likely to be something a charitable organisation would seek for itself, it might be useful to be aware of so that you can communicate these potential opportunities to your beneficiaries.

9 The activity of fundraising

What fundraisers actually do

When someone says that they spend a lot of time fundraising, this can mean a number of things.

One big distinction is between those who organise fundraising and those who actually do it. The first is often called fundraising management. It is often quite different from actually asking people for money, though many people do both. If you are not able to go out and introduce yourself to people, often strangers, and ask them to give money to your charity, do not despair. Your job can then be to organise things so that someone else, who enjoys it, does this asking.

A second distinction is between those who work mainly on paper, whose fundraising is primarily a desk job, and those who do the exact opposite, seldom putting finger to keyboard. The first may be, for example, a professional trust fundraiser – there are now hundreds of such people, to the dismay of many grant-makers – or a dedicated direct mail marketer. The personal fundraiser may spend their time talking to donors and potential donors, or with volunteers who are running fundraising events, a very different activity.

The point is that there is a need for all these activities. Unfortunately there is a tendency to get stuck in one groove. We find apparently similar charities that seek almost all their funding from grant-making charities, or from sponsored events or from individual donors, often pretty unaware that anyone else does differently. A good example is in the disability field. For historical reasons – they were pretty much the first in the field – charities for blind and partially sighted people, especially local ones, still tend to rely almost wholly on personal donations. Indeed they may have done so since the days of Queen Victoria. Other charities, often built around media publicity for an unfortunate particular case, may live almost wholly from the income from celebrity-backed, high-publicity events. Yet more, often created through specific statutory programmes, rely wholly on public money. They all often assume that what they do is the only 'normal' practice. It is not; there are choices.

Secrets of success

There are indeed 'born' fundraisers who simply go out and ask people for money, often with spectacular and continuing success – you have probably come across one or two of them. But they are few and far between and you do not have to be one of them in order to raise lots of money.

Success comes most easily to those who think carefully about the resources they have, usually in the form of the personal energy of the people committed to the cause, look at all the possible ways they could go, and then plan their fundraising to make the best of these opportunities, rather than just going off in the first direction that presents itself.

When people have set out their fundraising strategy, but found later that no money is coming in it is nearly always for the same reason – short-term pressures have meant that they have simply not got around to putting in the fundraising time. They are probably funded by short-term grants, or by unsatisfactory service agreements with statutory agencies. They knew that this was leaving them in a vulnerable position but the pressures of coping with the day-to-day needs of their beneficiaries have overwhelmed their plans to change this situation. And then, too often, they find they have left it too late and are facing an immediate crisis that fundraising, seldom a short-term activity, cannot resolve for them in the time available.

The good news is that those who have indeed formed a reasonable fundraising plan, and then put the necessary time and resources into implementing it, nearly always succeed. I hardly ever meet people who say that they have tried asking people for money, but they said 'No'.

Indeed the US fundraiser I quoted earlier seems to me to have got it right: 'I get money when I ask for it, and the more people I ask, the more I get'.

References

BIG (n.d.), 'About the Big Lottery Fund' [web page],
www.biglotteryfund.org.uk/about-big/our-approach/about-big-lottery-fund,
The Big Lottery Fund, accessed 25 May 2015

Botting Herbst, Nina and Michael Norton (2012), *The Complete Fundraising Handbook*, London, The Directory of Social Change

Burnett, Ken (1996), *Friends for Life: Relationship Fundraising in Practice*, London, White Lion Press

CAF (2015), Charity Trends [search tool], www.charitytrends.org/
SearchTool_Step1.aspx, accessed 27 April 2015

Dobbs, Joy, Véronique Jochum, Karl Wilding, Malcolm Smith and Richard Harrison (2012), *UK Giving*, London and West Malling, NCVO and CAF

DSC (2010), *Ineligible Applications: the Wasted Work of the Voluntary Sector*, London, Directory of Social Change

DSC (2015), Trust Funding [search tool], www.trustfunding.org.uk, The Directory of Social Change, accessed 18 March 2015

IoF (n.d.a), 'Fundraising Costs' [web page], www.institute-of-
fundraising.org.uk, Institute of Fundraising, accessed 14 January 2015

IoF (n.d.b), 'Data Protection', [web page], www.institute-of-
fundraising.org.uk/guidance/frequently-asked-fundraising-questions/data-
protection, Institute of Fundraising, accessed 29 January 2015

Kane, David, Joe Heywood and Pete Bass (2014), *The UK Civil Society Almanac 2014*, London, NCVO

Macmillan (n.d.), 'Coffee Morning' [home page], coffee.macmillan.org.uk,
Macmillan Cancer Support, accessed 14 January 2015

Norton, Michael and Murray Culshaw (2000), *Getting Started in Fundraising*, New Delhi, Sage Publications India

Ofcom (2014), 'Facts and figures' [web page], media.ofcom.org.uk/facts,
accessed 26 May 2015

Sherburn House (2014), *Christ's Hospital in Sherburn (Sherburn House Charity) Grants: Amended Guidance for applicants* [PDF publication], www.sherburnhouse.org/media/files/grant_guidelines_january_2014.pdf, accessed 11 February 2015

Townsend, Lucy (2014), 'How much has the ice bucket challenge achieved?', www.bbc.co.uk/news/magazine-29013707, BBC, accessed 29 January 2015

UK Community Foundations (2015), 'Helping Build Thriving Communities' [home page], ukcommunityfoundations.org, accessed 22 May 2015

Virgin (n.d.), 'Run for Charity' [web page], www.virginmoneylondonmarathon.com/en-gb/charity/run-charity, Virgin Money London Marathon, accessed 11 February 2015

Wikipedia (2014), 'Race for Life' [web page], en.wikipedia.org, Wikimedia Foundation, accessed 14 January 2015

Useful organisations

To contact these organisations by email or online form, please visit the website listed.

Charity regulators
Charity Commission for England and Wales

Website: www.gov.uk/government/organisations/charity-commission
Tel: 0845 3000 218

Charity Commission for Northern Ireland

Website: www.charitycommissionni.org.uk
Tel: 028 3832 0220

Office of the Scottish Charity Regulator (OSCR)

Website: www.oscr.org.uk
Tel: 01382 220446

Other useful organisations
ACEVO

Website: www.acevo.org.uk
Tel: 020 7014 4600 (members only)

Association of Fundraising Consultants (AFC)

Website: www.afc.org.uk
Tel: 07932 101058

CAF – Charities Aid Foundation

Website: www.cafonline.org
Tel: 03000 123 000 (head office)

Directory of Social Change (DSC)

Website: www.dsc.org.uk
Tel: 08450 77 77 07

The Fundraising Standards Board

Website: www.frsb.org.uk
Tel: 0333 321 8803

HM Revenue & Customs Charities

Website: www.gov.uk/government/organisations/hm-revenue-customs/
services-information
Tel: 0300 123 1073

Institute of Fundraising

Website: www.institute-of-fundraising.org.uk
Tel: 020 7840 1000

National Association of Voluntary and Community Action (NAVCA)

Website: www.navca.org.uk
Tel: 0114 278 6636

NCVO (National Council of Voluntary Organisations)

Website: www.ncvo.org.uk
Tel: 020 7713 6161

NICVA (Northern Ireland Council for Voluntary Action)

Website: www.nicva.org
Tel: 028 9087 7777

SCVO (Scottish Council for Voluntary Organisations)

Website: www.scvo.org.uk
Tel: 0131 474 8000

Small Charities Coalition (SCC)

Website: www.smallcharities.org.uk
Tel: 020 7358 6490 (Mondays and Thursdays 10am–2pm only)

WCVA (Wales Council for Voluntary Action)

Website: www.wcva.org.uk
Tel: 0800 2888 329

Index